Helping Children Who Are Blind

Family and community support for children with vision problems

Written by Sandy Niemann
and Namita Jacob

Illustrated by Heidi Broner

The Hesperian Foundation
Berkeley, California, USA

First edition: September 2000.

Printed in the USA.

ISBN: 0-942364-34-1

Library of Congress Cataloging-in-Publication Data

Niemann, Sandy.

  Helping children who are blind : family and community support for children with vision problems / written by Sandy Niemann and Namita Jacob; illustrated by Heidi Broner -- 1st ed.

     p. cm.

  ISBN 0-942364-34-1 (paper)

  1. Children, Blind -- Family relationships. 2. Visually handicapped children -- Family relationships. 3. Children, Blind -- Services for. 4. Visually handicapped children -- Services for. 5. Child development. I. Jacob, Namita. II. Title.

HV1596.4.N54 2000

362.4'18'083-dc21

00-058209

Cover photograph by
Namita Jacob of a blind boy
and his sister in Vagash,
Gujarat, India.

Cover art: anonymous tribal
design, Orissa, India.

The Hesperian Foundation
PO Box 11577
Berkeley, California 94712-2577 United States of America

Credits and Thanks

The Hesperian Foundation is especially grateful to the committed health staff of Plan International. They have been important collaborators, sharing their understanding of the needs of parents and health promoters working with children. Plan International staff in Bangladesh reviewed and field-tested early versions of this book, improving it immeasurably. In addition, Plan's US member, Childreach, is generously helping fund the development of this series.

Project coordinator:
Doreen Greenstein

Art coordination:
Sandy Niemann

Design and production:
Christine Sienkiewicz,
Lora Santiago

Cover design:
Christine Sienkiewicz

Additional writing:
Doreen Greenstein,
Sarah Shannon, Todd Jailer,
Susan McCallister, Aryn Faur

Research assistance:
Kinkini Banerjee, Felicia Lester, Amina LaCour Mini, Rebecca Ratcliff, Nicolle Perez, Shana Nelson, Karen Cook

Production management:
Susan McCallister

Field-testing and networking:
Estelle Schneider, Denise Bergez, Rebecca Ratcliff, Sofia Betancourt

Additional illustrations:
Christine Sienkiewicz, Lora Santiago, Petra Röhr-Rouendaal

Additional production:
Sofia Betancourt, Nicolle Perez

Copy editing:
Jane Maxwell

Proofreading: Lorraine Mann

Editorial oversight:
Todd Jailer

A special thanks to all the funders of this book and the Early Assistance Series:

Childreach, the US member of Plan International
DANIDA - Royal Danish Ministry of Foreign Affairs
Frank Edwards
Morgan Hill Lions Club
The Presiding Bishop's Fund for World Relief (Episcopal Church)
Scales of Justice Lions Club
May and Stanley Smith Charitable Trust
United Nations Children's Fund (UNICEF)
United Nations Voluntary Fund on Disability

Credits and Thanks

Field Test Sites

This book was developed in collaboration with grassroots organizations and parents groups around the world. We gratefully acknowledge the contribution of those involved in the field-testing process:

Arthur Blaxall School, South Africa

Association of Early Intervention, Czech Republic

Belize Council for the Visually Impaired, Belize

Blind Babies Foundation, USA

Blind People's Association, India

Community Disability Program, Institute of Child Health, UK

Development Partners, Bangladesh

Hilton/Perkins Program, Thailand

Jamaica Society for the Blind, Jamaica

KAMPI (National Federation of Organizations of Persons with Disabilities), Philippines

Institute for the Blind, South Africa

Laramara, Brazil

National Association of the Blind, India

Nepal Association for the Welfare of the Blind, Nepal

St. Lucia Blind Welfare Association, St. Lucia

Sight Savers International, Kenya

Special Education Organization, Islamic Republic of Iran

Uganda National Institute of Special Education, Uganda

Uganda Society for Disabled Children, Uganda

Wa School for the Blind, Ghana

Advisors and reviewers

This book was written with the guidance of many people around the world. We wish to express our thanks to the many advisors and reviewers who shared their knowledge and expertise:

Tayyab Afghani, Al-Shifa Trust Hospital, Pakistan

Nancy Akeson

Carolina Arnold, Save the Children, Nepal

Pam Bondy

Jonathan Brakarsh, Family Support Trust, Zimbabwe

Freda Briggs

Ellen vor der Bruegge

Joan Carey, Save the Children, UK

Mike Collins, Hilton/Perkins Program, USA

Tara Dikeman

Birgit Dyssegaard, DANIDA

Marvin Efron

Roxanna Pastor Fasquelle

Suzanne Gilbert, SEVA, USA

Teresa Glass

Srilakshmi Guruja

Gulbadan Habibi, UNICEF

Tessa Hamblin

Marci Hanson, San Francisco State University

Sally Hartley

Ralf Hotchkiss

Khairul Islam, Plan International, Bangladesh

Penny May Kaman

Jenny Kern

Amanda Luek

David Morley

Dan Perlman

Julie Bernas Pierce, Blind Babies Foundation, USA

Sherry Raynor, Blind Children's Fund, USA

Sandra Rosen

Lesley Sternin and A.E. Tong-Summerford, Parental Stress Services, USA

Aminuzzaman Talukder, Helen Keller International, Bangladesh

Catherine Thomas

Marigold Thorburn

Sheila Wirz, Centre for International Child Health, UK

Irene Yen

Medical reviewers

Davida Coady

Gustavo González

Lesli Handmacher

Brian Linde

John Pratt-Johnson

*We would like to thank the participants in the South Asian translators meeting (New Delhi, August, 2000), for their comments on "Chapter 12: Preventing Sexual Abuse." Thanks also to the Voluntary Health Association of India for permission to adapt the story on page 117 from their book, **Child Abuse: A Growing Concern** (1993).*

Contents

HOW TO USE THIS BOOK

When using this book, try to read Chapters 1 through 4 first. These chapters have important background information on how to help your child learn. Then turn to Chapters 5 through 8, and Chapters 10 and 11, to find examples of activities to help your child learn new skills.

The remainder of this book contains information to help caregivers support one another, to help parents learn from one another and work together, and to increase your knowledge of blindness and vision problems.

ABOUT THE PICTURES

Since this book was written for people around the world who care for children with vision problems, the drawings show people from many cultures. We hope these drawings will remind you that people all over the world face the same challenges you do.

A NOTE ABOUT THE LANGUAGE WE USE IN THIS BOOK

Most books about children who are blind talk about the children as if they are all boys and use the word "he" to refer to any child. This happens because society holds men to be more important than women and that belief is built into our language.

In fact, girls are not only left out of our language, they often receive less attention and care as well. This can include getting less food and getting less health care — both of which contribute to blindness.

In a small way, we have tried to reflect a more equal world by using both "he" and "she" to refer to children. Because "he-or-she" is awkward, we use "he" in some chapters and "she" in others.

Remember, all children need and deserve our love and support.

Chapter 1

How Can I Help My Child?

The Stories of Kamala and Rani

Kamala

Kamala and her parents Suma and Anil live in a small village in southern India. When Kamala was very young, her parents noticed that she never reached for the toys they offered her. So they took her to the doctor in a nearby town to see what was wrong.

The doctor told them that Kamala was almost blind. She could see some movement and the difference between light and dark, but nothing more. "Her sight will not get better," the doctor said. Suma and Anil returned home, very sad. "How could this have happened?" Suma thought. "She is such a nice child." Suma was sad for a long time.

Kamala is blind, but your other children can see.

Try to think of other things.

Suma, you have been crying for months.

Suma and Anil cared for Kamala the best they could.

Because Anil's work did not pay enough to feed his family, Suma and her 2 older daughters made clothes to sell at the market. There was little time to play with Kamala while the family worked, and she spent most of the day sitting quietly in the corner. Sometimes Suma worried that Kamala rarely moved or made sounds, but she also was relieved that Kamala seemed content just being near them.

By the time Kamala was 3, she knew only a few words. She seemed to be lost in her own world most of the time, making strange movements like poking her eyes or flapping her hands. She could not feed or dress herself. It was faster for Suma to do these things for her.

Because Kamala did not play as other children her age did, and had not learned to care for herself, her arms and legs never grew strong. When other children her age were learning to stand and walk, Kamala's legs were too weak to support her weight.

When she was old enough to start school, Kamala's parents carried her to the schoolhouse. But school frightened her, because she had never been away from home. Day after day Kamala sat in class and cried. If the teacher spoke to her she would not answer. Finally, Suma and Anil decided that school was not helping Kamala and stopped taking her. But they worried about her future. "If she can't get an education, how will she live? Who will take care of her when we are gone?"

Rani

Rani is a little blind girl, born in another village in India. When her parents Jeevan and Aruna learned their baby was blind, Rani's grandmother Baka said, "We should do everything we can to teach this baby. Look at me. I lost my sight 5 years ago. I can still do most of the things I used to do. I still bring water from the well. I still milk the goats."

"But you could already do all those things before you went blind," Jeevan replied. "How could a blind baby learn?"

"We must help her learn," Baka answered him. "Just as I've learned to do things by sound and touch, so Rani must learn."

The health worker suggested they give Rani lots of objects to play with, and encourage her to use her hearing, touch, and smell to make up for what she could not see. "And talk to her a lot," the health worker said.

Baka, especially, had Rani touch and listen to everything. She played games with her and sang to her. When Rani was 2, Baka taught her to feel her way along the walls and fence, just as she did. By age 3, Rani could find her own way to the latrine and the well.

That's a banana, Rani. Feel how smooth it is.

Can you smell it, Rani? A ripe banana smells sweet.

Jeevan, Aruna, and Baka did not have a lot of time to do special activities with Rani. They worked long hours in their small shop. But they helped Rani learn new skills by including her in what they were already doing, like going to the market. These simple, everyday activities made a big difference in helping Rani develop many skills.

When Rani started school, the local children came for her every day. When the villagers saw them all walking down the road together, it was hard to tell which child was blind.

Understanding the stories of Kamala and Rani

If your child cannot see well or is blind, you can help her learn many skills, just as Rani's family helped her. But it is important to understand why Rani was able to learn the skills other children her age were learning while Kamala did not learn them.

To understand this, it helps to know:
- how children develop (learn new skills as they grow)
- how difficulty seeing affects development

How children develop

Every child develops in 3 main areas: physical (body), mental (thinking), and social (talking, listening, and getting along with other people). In each area, a child learns new skills step by step in a certain order.

Before a child can learn to walk, for example, he must first learn many simple kinds of body control:

① First, he needs to be able to hold his head up and to move his arms and legs.

② Then he can use his arms and legs to lift himself to sit.

③ While sitting, he begins to reach, lean, and twist. This helps him develop balance – a skill he will soon need for standing and walking.

④ Then he pulls himself up to a standing position.

Before a child can have a conversation with other people, he needs to learn many simple communication skills like:

Give it to me, please.

① **understanding simple words and requests**

② **using signs or gestures**

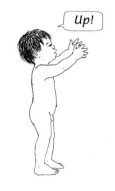

Up!

③ **saying simple words**

Smells good.

④ **using short sentences**

Each new skill a child learns builds on the skills he already knows and prepares him to learn other, more difficult skills. So when a child does not learn a skill, this means he not only has problems with that skill, but with other skills that depend on it.

For example, if he has a problem holding up his head, he will then have difficulty learning skills like sitting or crawling in which holding up the head is important. Over time, his development begins to fall behind other children his age.

Each new skill builds on already-learned skills, like building blocks.

How vision problems affect development

When a child can see, she usually develops skills 'naturally' as she watches and plays with the people and objects she sees around her.

Playing gives a child many 'natural' opportunities to move about and to learn.

When a child sees an interesting object, she reaches for it or crawls to get it. This helps her arms and legs grow strong.

Playing with objects helps a child learn thinking skills, like solving simple problems. Here a child learns how to bring her toy closer by pulling its string.

beads

Playing also helps a child to talk. When she is interested in objects, she learns to name them.

Children naturally copy what they see. Watching other people helps a child learn how to do things and how to behave.

A young child learns to speak by hearing other people speak and by seeing what they talk about.

A child learns how to dress himself by watching other people.

A child who cannot see well has fewer 'natural' opportunities to learn. So he may learn skills more slowly than children who see, and his development may begin to fall behind.

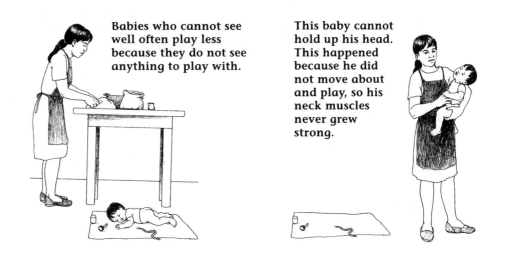

Babies who cannot see well often play less because they do not see anything to play with.

This baby cannot hold up his head. This happened because he did not move about and play, so his neck muscles never grew strong.

His social development may begin to fall behind as well.

Papa let me ride with him yesterday. We went fast!

A child who cannot see well may not understand or take part in conversations because he cannot see what is being talked about.

So he may begin to spend a lot of time alone because he does not understand what others are saying.

Most of these problems do not have to happen. Children who cannot see can learn to use their other senses — their sense of hearing, touch, smell, and taste — to help them understand their world and to learn what other children usually learn by seeing.

How you can help

Helping young children develop all areas of their body and mind through planned opportunities to experience, explore and play with things is called 'stimulation' or 'early assistance.' In this book you will find many simple activities that can be done as you play with your child or as you do your daily work. You can also adapt these activities so they fit with your child and your daily life. For example:

What's making that noise?

If you get your baby's attention with a noisy toy and show him the sound it makes...

What a big noise, Oscar! Listen! I can make a noise just like you.

...he will be more interested in playing. He will also learn to pay attention to sounds and where they come from.

That's the tire, Yaso. When the bike goes, the tire goes around.

If you encourage a child to use his sense of touch, hearing, and smell to find out what objects are like...

I'm riding too!

...he will learn more about the world and be able to talk about what he knows.

If you do these kinds of activities often, your child will have a childhood as full of fun and learning as any other child. As he grows up he can learn to:

Louis is such a big boy now...look how he gets around!

move about by himself

Pull Sam, we're winning!

play with other children

Pat the soil down all around the plant

help with the family's work

I know the answer to that question, Mrs. Natomo.

go to school or learn a trade

What about my child's future?

Many parents worry about their child's future, even after he begins to learn new skills and go to school. They wonder, "What will happen when he grows up? How will he manage when we are gone?"

Sometimes it helps parents to learn about others who, even though they cannot see, have grown up to lead full and satisfying lives — to have families of their own, to earn a living, and to become respected members of their communities. Blind people can achieve this when:

- people understand that blind children, like all children, can learn.
- their families and communities help them succeed.

Here, for example, is what the future held for Rani:

As Rani grew up, she often helped her parents in their shop. By the time she had finished school, Rani was so good at math she was able to help with the store's accounts. She also kept track of supplies by writing the lists in Braille. Rani's parents were pleased with her accomplishments.

When Rani turned 18 her parents accepted a proposal of marriage from Mani, a young man from their village. Mani and Rani were married, and after Rani had her first baby, she kept the baby beside her as she worked at the shop.

How proud I am of Rani.

Rani was so capable, people began to rely on her skills in other ways.

We've seen you manage your accounts. Can you teach us too?

Children asked her to help with their school work. "Rani usually knows the answer," they said. And when some neighbor women started a weaving cooperative, they came to Rani for help setting up their accounts.

Sometimes Rani thinks about her life and how it might have been different if she could see. "Perhaps I would have done less if I could see," she says. "Being blind made me determined to have a life just like other people."

Chapter 2

Getting Started

A baby starts learning as soon as she is born. In the first 5 years, she will learn more skills, and learn them more quickly and easily, than at any other time in her life. So it is important to begin early assistance activities as soon as possible.

You may find it difficult, though, to know how to begin doing these activities with your child. This chapter is designed to help you get started and contains information on:

- making the best use of the information in this book
- deciding which activities to do first
- fitting these activities into your family's daily life

How can this book help?

In this book, we give information, reasons for doing things, ideas, and suggestions. You can use this book to:

- understand more about blindness and child development.
- learn the reasons for doing each activity. This will make it easier for you to create other activities that accomplish the same goals.
- learn from others parents who have raised children with vision problems.
- develop and carry out learning activities that work best for you and your child.

Which activities should I do first?

Parents often think they need special training to plan early assistance activities for their child. But this is not so. As a parent, you know more about your child than anyone else. To decide what activities to do first, start by asking yourself questions like these:

Are there things my child cannot do that other children her age are doing?

Almost all children Amina's age are walking. I want to help her learn.

If so, your child probably needs special help learning these skills. Choosing activities that build these skills can help a child catch up with other children.

Are there areas of my child's development that I am particularly concerned about?

These might be ways your child lags behind other children, or they might be areas of development that are especially important to you or your family.

Ali is so quiet and we're such a talkative family. I worry he'll be left out.

For more information on the ages and order in which children usually learn new skills, see the Child Development Charts beginning on page 176.

FINDING ACTIVITIES THAT CAN HELP

Once you have identified areas in which your child needs help, look at the Table of Contents on page 5 to find the chapter of the book that covers this area of development. Each chapter contains information and activities to help your child learn new skills. For example:

The chapter on movement should help me help Amina learn to walk.

I'll read the communication chapter to learn how to help Ali begin to talk.

The first activities in each chapter help a child learn the most simple skills in that area of development. Once a child has learned these skills, she can begin working on the more difficult skills described later in the chapter. If your child can already do some of the skills described, start working on the skills immediately following those she knows. If she does not know any of the skills, then start at the beginning of the chapter.

Try to work on skills in the order they appear in the chapter. This is important because children develop skills step-by-step, in a certain order. **Trying to teach your child an advanced skill before she has learned the smaller, simpler skills that come first can lead to disappointment for both you and your child.**

How can I fit these activities into my family's daily life?

It is important to think about how to do early assistance activities in ways that do not make more work for you. By making everyday activities into learning experiences, teaching your child will be easier for you and will not take extra time.

Explain the sounds and smells to your child when you go to the market.

Talk about what you are doing as you work.

MANY PEOPLE CAN HELP DO THESE ACTIVITIES

Encourage family members, neighbors, and friends to become involved, too. People around you often want to help, but they may feel uncomfortable because they do not know how. Share what you have learned about vision problems, the activities you and your child are working on, and the reasons for doing these activities.

I worried I wouldn't have time to teach my son Guddi. But between myself, my husband and the other children, we have found many ways to do things with him as we go about our chores.

My mother-in-law and neighbors also help with our daughter. At first they thought it would be hard because they weren't sure what to do. I explained what Namita needed to learn and how to help her, and now they spend time with her every day.

Children can also help if you show them how. Explain how they can adapt some of their games to include your child. Then encourage them to come up with new ideas on their own.

The children have discovered that Hanke can follow them when they clap their hands. Now they can all play tag.

Chapter 3

General Guidelines for Learning Activities

This chapter describes some of the general guidelines parents have found helpful when teaching their child new skills. Try using these guidelines in addition to the specific instructions for each activity in Chapters 5 through 8, and Chapters 10 and 11.

You are the expert about your child

No one knows your child and his abilities as well as you do. Listen to your feelings and experiences about how your child is doing, even if they are different from what a doctor, health worker, teacher or this book is telling you. You can learn a lot from people who have experience with children who have vision problems, but every child is different. You are the expert about your child.

Let your child take the lead

Play is an important way for children to learn about the world. A child is most eager to play when he is doing something he likes. So if your child shows interest in an object, person, or activity, use his play to help him learn new skills.

Letting your child take the lead helps him learn that his choices are important and that he has some control over what happens. But it does not mean that everything is unplanned. You need to think about the skills your child needs to learn (see page 12), and the kinds of activities and objects that can help him learn these skills. Then you can think of ways to help him learn more while he is playing.

Adapt activities for your child

A child can learn a certain skill in many different ways. You can adapt the activities in this book to best suit your child, your family and your community.

As you do activities with your child, you will find ways of doing things that interest him and make him want to do something...

...and you will learn what upsets him or makes him want to stop.

Noah seems to be afraid to slide by himself. But maybe he will be willing to try sliding if I stand nearby and talk to him.

I don't have blocks but these cans are just as good.

You can adapt activities to make use of materials you already have. For example, if an activity in this book shows a child using a toy, you do not need to make or buy that same toy. Instead, use whatever is readily available.

Adapt activities so they fit in with your daily work and your family's activities.

The book said to help Visit strengthen his hands. Arranging the fruits at our market stand will help him and help me too.

First, try activities yourself

As you prepare to teach your child, try each activity yourself, thinking about each step. This will help you think of the best way to teach your child.

This father is learning how to feed himself without being able to see.

This father is learning how to feed himself when he can see only the area off to the side.

Work from behind your child

Yaso, can I put my hands on yours to help you?

When you are showing your child how to do a new activity, like feeding or dressing himself, it may be easier for him to understand your movements if you are behind him. Sometimes it works well to put your hands over his. But be sure to ask him first if it is okay.

Be consistent

Try to teach a skill in the same way each time, using the same words and steps. You will need to do different kinds of activities because children do not stay interested in one thing for very long. But try not to change the way you talk about and teach each skill. It also helps to begin and end activities with the same words or actions. This way a child will know that the activity is changing.

Supper is over, Pepe.

Pepe's father says these words each time the family finishes supper.

Allow your child enough time

A child who has difficulty seeing takes longer to do things, at least at first. He needs time to think about what you have asked him to do and about how he will respond. So be sure to give him enough time to be successful at what he does.

He always waits a few moments before he begins to eat.

Let your child know how he is doing

A child who does not see well cannot see how close he is to completing a task, so he needs you to let him know. Otherwise he may get discouraged, not realizing how much he has already done. And be sure to tell him when he does something well. All children need praise.

Good, Kofi. You have only one more button to do.

Hear the water? I'm washing the floor, Kam San. It gets dirty after everyone walks on it.

Let your child know what is happening around him

A child who can see knows a lot about what is happening around him. He knows, for example, who is in the room, who is talking, what other people are doing, and where sounds come from. A blind child learns to use his senses to know many of these same things. You can help him learn about his surroundings by describing and showing him what is going on.

Remember how children learn

When you are teaching a child a new skill, he will learn it in stages.

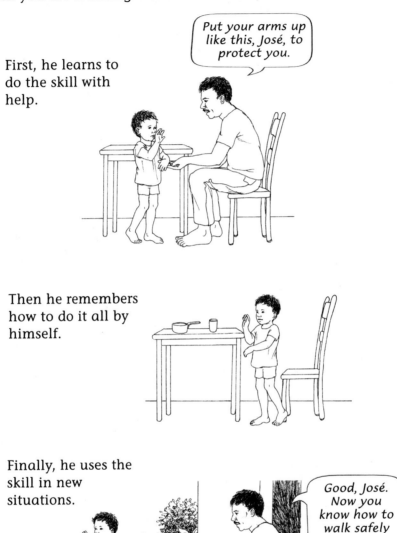

First, he learns to do the skill with help.

Put your arms up like this, José, to protect you.

Then he remembers how to do it all by himself.

Finally, he uses the skill in new situations.

Good, José. Now you know how to walk safely outside, too.

Try to be aware of all 3 stages as you teach your child. Remember, also, that all children need a lot of practice before they completely learn a new skill.

Many of the activities in this book need you to give your child a lot of help at first. But as he begins to master a skill, give him less and less help. For example, when your child is learning to feed himself:

At first you may put your hands over his hands and move his arms.

Kofi, here come the yams.

As you feel him start to do some of the activity himself, loosen your hold on his hand. Then gradually move your hand to his wrist and lower arm...

I'm putting my hand on your arm to give you a little help.

...and then to his elbow.

That's it, Kofi. You are starting to feed yourself.

Encourage your child to be independent

It is natural to want to help your child do things. But be careful about helping your child so much that he does not have a chance to learn how the world works. For example:

When a child drops a toy, it is natural to want to pick it up and give it to him...

You almost have it, Dong Dong. Just move your hand a little closer to the tapping sound...

...but he will learn more if you help him find the toy himself.

Make the best use of your child's remaining sight

If your child can see a little, try to do activities that make use of his remaining sight. The next chapter explains how.

Since Norma seems to see things better in bright light, I'll put her on a blanket with her toys here in the patio while I wash the clothes.

Chapter 4
Finding Out What Your Child Can See

Many children who have difficulty seeing are not totally blind but can see a little. Some children can see the difference between light and dark but cannot see any objects. Other children can see objects if they are in certain places, in certain kinds of light, or if they are a certain size or a bright color. Some children can see movement.

Before starting the activities in this book, it is important to find out what your child can see. Knowing this will help you do activities in ways that **will help her learn most.**

If your child can see a little, knowing how she sees best also means you can choose activities that **will help her make the most of her remaining sight.**

I was afraid that Simi would strain her eyes and might lose what little sight she has. But it hasn't hurt her a bit and now she uses her sight to help her move around and play!

Using vision does not lead to its loss. Your child's eyes will not be hurt if she uses her sight to help her do things.

Is my child totally blind, or can she see a little?

If you are unsure whether your child has some sight, watch to see:

Does she close her eyes in bright sunlight or turn her head toward a light?

Does she bring objects close to her eyes?

Does she follow slowly moving objects with her head?

Does she always tilt her head in a certain way?

Does she move her hand back and forth in front of her eyes?

Does she reach for objects that do not make sounds?

If you notice any of these things, you can learn more about what they mean by reading the next few pages.

What does my child see?

WHAT KIND OF LIGHT HELPS MY CHILD SEE BEST?

Some children may have trouble adjusting to changes in the amount of light. Or your child may be able to see in some kinds of light but not others.

Notice if your child squints or turns away from light. She may see best when the light is not too bright or when the weather is cloudy.

Notice if your child likes to look at things in bright light. She may see best in brightly lit rooms or strong sunlight.

The direction the light comes from may affect what your child can see. Try changing the position of the light as she does different tasks to find out what helps her see best.

To see small details, this child sees best when the light is directly over the object.

The kind of light may also make a difference. Some children do well with light focused on what they see. Others do well with light that is spread out but still strong.

AT WHAT DISTANCE DOES MY CHILD SEE BEST?

Most children who can see a little see objects best that are about an arm's length away. But some children see an object best when it is very close to their face. Others see best when an object is much farther away. Watch your child carefully to see how far she likes to hold objects from her face. This is probably the distance at which she sees best.

This child sees objects best when they are about an arm's length away...

...but this child sees objects best when they are close up.

IN WHAT DIRECTION DOES MY CHILD SEE BEST?

Although most children see objects that are directly in front of them most clearly, they can also see objects that are off to either side, or above or below their eyes. Sometimes, however, a child cannot see very far to the side. Or she may not be able to see certain areas at all, like the area directly in front of her, on either side, or below her chin or above her eyes. To find out what direction your child sees best, watch her closely to see where she likes to hold objects or the way she tilts her head to look at an object.

This child can only see objects that are off to the side. To see an object, she must move her head to the side and look back at the object.

WHAT SIZE OBJECTS DOES MY CHILD SEE BEST?

Most children who can see a little see large objects best. But some children can see only a small area in front of them. These children will recognize small objects more easily than large ones. Watch your child to see the sizes of objects she likes to play with.

This child likes to play with small things because she sees them best.

This child sees large objects best.

DOES MY CHILD KNOW HOW FAR AWAY OBJECTS ARE?

Some children have difficulty judging how far away an object is. So when they reach for the object, they may reach too far. Or they may not reach far enough, because they think the object is closer than it really is. To find out if your child can judge distance, watch to see if she reaches correctly for toys or other objects.

This child thinks the bottle is farther away than it really is.

This child likes playing with the dark colored pan because she can see it better than the spoon.

DOES MY CHILD LIKE CERTAIN COLORS OR THE DIFFERENCE (CONTRAST) BETWEEN CERTAIN COLORS?

Some children can see objects when they are brightly colored, or when they are against a different colored background. Watch to see if your child prefers certain colors, differences between colors, or patterns. These are probably the colors and patterns she sees best.

WHAT ELSE AFFECTS MY CHILD'S SIGHT?

A child often seems to see better at some times than at others. This does not mean her sight has changed, but that something else is affecting how much she sees, such as:

- whether an object is familiar to her
- how tired she is
- her health
- whether she is taking medicines
- whether she is feeling happy or sad

You will probably need to watch your child carefully in different situations and at different times to find out what she can really see.

Helping your child use the sight she has

If your child can see a little:

Give her lots of different objects to look at. This will encourage her to become interested in the world around her and to use her sight more.

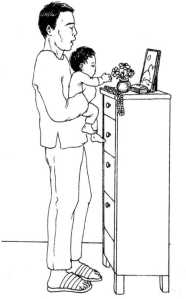

One way to show her different objects is to walk around the house. Talk about what you see, and encourage her to touch and hold things.

Let your child hold things or move her body in the way that helps her see best, even if it looks awkward to you. For example:

If your child sees only a small area in front of her, she will see more if she looks up, down, and to the right and left as she moves instead of straight ahead.

If your child can see a little, try changing the amount of light, the kind of light, or the direction the light comes from. See what works best.

If she has trouble seeing when the amount of light changes, teach her to stop moving and to wait for her eyes to adjust.

Notice if your child tends to pay attention to certain:

- colors
- patterns
- sizes
- color contrasts

If she does, you can use these preferences to help her learn and move about safely.

To catch her baby's interest, this mother rolls a brightly colored ball across a white cloth.

Use bright colors to mark the edges of objects or places. This will help her learn to recognize places and shapes.

Here's the yellow ribbon. This is my friend José's door.

When she is older, brightly colored ribbons, cloths, or objects can help her know where she is.

Brightly colored tape or paint can help a child know when the height of the floor changes.

Will my child's sight get worse?

To answer this question, you will need to know what causes your child's difficulty seeing. For more information, see the chapter "Why Children Lose Their Vision and What We Can Do", page 155.

Chapter 5
Activities for the Young Baby
(Birth to 6 Months)

A new baby does not usually look as though she is doing very much. She spends most of her time eating, sleeping, and resting. But even though she may not seem aware of her surroundings, a new baby is already starting to learn about her world. She does this by using her senses: hearing, touch, smell, taste, and sight.

A baby who is blind or who cannot see well also begins learning as soon as she is born. But she needs your help to introduce her to a world she cannot see.

You can help by giving her many opportunities to listen, feel, and smell. Encourage her to explore and play.

If a baby cannot see toys or people's faces, she does not know that there is an interesting world to explore.

That's a spoon, Rosa. It's fun to play with.

She needs your help to find that out.

As you do activities with your baby, talk to her. Even if you think she is too young to understand the words you say, remember that listening to a person's voice is one of the main ways she will learn about the world. For information on communicating with your baby as you do these activities, see the chapter on "Communication", page 45.

Irene is so tiny. She sleeps and nurses, and then she sleeps again.

Isn't it amazing how much babies change in their first few months? Look at Marcos, he pays attention to everything. When his big sister comes into the room, he sits up and reaches for her to hold him.

Hector can almost sit up but he isn't as strong as Marcos. I was so worried about his blindness at first, but he has done a lot of growing in his own way. And he knows his sister's voice, too. He always wants her to hold him whenever he hears her nearby.

ACTIVITIES

The activities in this chapter are divided into 2 parts: for babies from birth to 3 months old and for babies 4 to 6 months old. These are the ages when babies can begin to work on the skills described here. But remember that it can take months for a baby to learn a new skill. So you may want to work on a few skills at a time. And remember that each baby will learn at her own pace.

BIRTH TO 3 MONTHS OLD

In the first 3 months of life, a baby can learn to:

- recognize familiar voices and sounds
- make noises other than crying
- discover her hands and feet
- lift her head
- tell the difference between smells
- touch and hold objects
- enjoy different kinds of touch
- help calm herself down

▶ To help your baby learn to trust people and her surroundings

A baby who can see soon learns that certain sounds, touches, and smells come from different people or objects. This helps her make sense of the world, feel secure in it, and want to explore it. But sounds, touches, and smells can frighten a blind baby because they seem to come from nowhere. She needs extra help to understand and feel secure in her surroundings.

You can help her understand where sounds and things that feel different come from. Help her know that learning about them can be fun.

Yes, it's your Papa! Do you feel my moustache?

Since your baby may not see what is about to happen, she needs you to let her know what will happen next. For example:

Touch her leg gently before changing her diaper (nappy). Tell her what you are about to do. Soon she will know what to expect when she feels the touch on her leg.

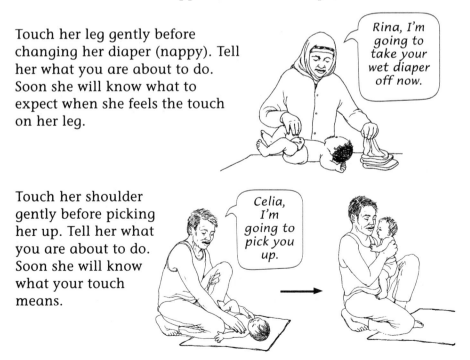

Rina, I'm going to take your wet diaper off now.

Touch her shoulder gently before picking her up. Tell her what you are about to do. Soon she will know what your touch means.

Celia, I'm going to pick you up.

▶ *To encourage your baby to respond to people and to sounds*

Keep your baby near you when she is awake. Speak to her often to let her know you are near. She will learn to recognize your voice and respond to it.

Radha, hear that noise? I'm cutting wheat.

Encourage family members to talk with her about what they are doing. If the same person always does the same activity — like giving the baby a bath — she will begin to recognize members of the family by what they do.

Next I'll wash your arm, Alba.

Who's my little sweet girl?

Encourage your baby to smile by talking to her. She may smile again if you blow softly on her belly or play with her toes.

Sing and play music for your baby. If she makes sounds, imitate them to encourage her to use her voice.

ga...ga... ...ga

When your baby begins to make sounds, play with her by putting her hands on your mouth and throat while you repeat the sounds. This also helps her learn where sounds come from.

▶ To help your baby become aware of her hands and legs, and to use her hands to hold objects

When feeding your baby, gently push upward on your baby's arm so that she puts her hand on your breast. This helps her get ready to hold objects. Feeding is also a good time to talk or sing to your baby.

♫ Ya ya me la la...

Try tying a toy that makes noise — like a small bell, seed pod, or bracelet — on her wrist or ankle. She will try to find the sound with her other hand and play with it.

Put your baby on her side with a cloth behind her back for support. She will naturally bring her hands together to play.

Remember, since small objects can choke a baby, you should stop her if she tries to put small toys or objects all the way into her mouth.

Give her things to hold that will feel different from each other when she touches them, like a piece of smooth, silky cloth and a rough cloth. You can also encourage her to pull on objects like a strong string of beads or a knotted cord. If you pull back slightly, she may pull harder.

Be careful she does not choke on the beads or swallow them.

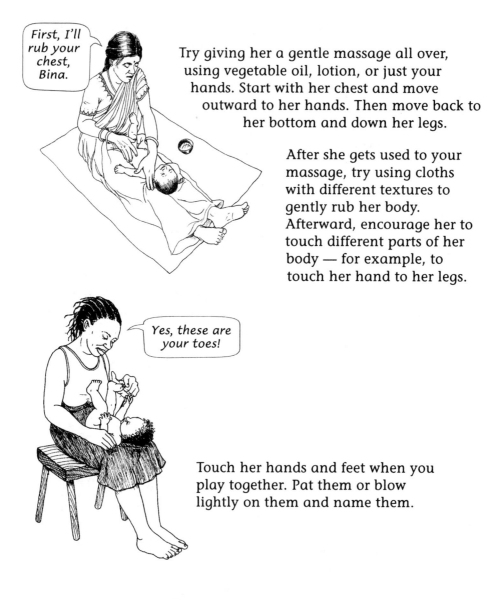

Try giving her a gentle massage all over, using vegetable oil, lotion, or just your hands. Start with her chest and move outward to her hands. Then move back to her bottom and down her legs.

After she gets used to your massage, try using cloths with different textures to gently rub her body. Afterward, encourage her to touch different parts of her body — for example, to touch her hand to her legs.

Touch her hands and feet when you play together. Pat them or blow lightly on them and name them.

▶ *To help your baby develop control of her head*

A baby's neck muscles grow strong when she lies on her stomach and lifts her head. A baby who can see will lift her head up to look at things, but a baby who cannot see will need other reasons to lift her head. Many babies may not like to lie on their stomachs. Your child may be more willing to do this if you:

Place your baby on your chest. If her face is near your face, she will want to lift her head when she hears your voice, or she will want to touch your face. You can also hold your arms around her and rock back and forth.

Put your baby over your knees, while supporting her with your hand. Rock her by moving your knees. This is an easy way to hold your child and encourages her to lift her head and strengthens her neck muscles. It also helps her prepare to crawl.

Let your baby feel a noisy toy, then shake it about 15 centimeters (6 inches) above her head. She will often lift her head to pay attention to the sound.

▶ *To help your baby explore objects through taste and smell*

Babies first learn about the world by tasting and exploring objects with their mouths. This is especially important for children who cannot see well because they must learn a lot through their other senses. Everything the baby plays with should be clean, and big enough so the baby will not choke.

Lightly touch your finger to your baby's mouth. Let her suck on your finger and explore it.

This is mama's finger, little one.

So Alita, do you like Tia Ana's spoon?

When your baby can hold objects by herself, encourage her to explore their smell and taste.

▶ *To help your baby feel different kinds of touch*

Play a game by dipping parts of her body in water, naming each part.

That's your hand in the water, Mei Mei.

This is a flower, Aminah. Smells good, doesn't it?

Encourage her to touch things with an interesting feel and a strong but pleasant smell — like fruits, vegetables, or flowers.

▶ *To help your baby get ready to roll over*

A baby who can see learns to roll over as she reaches for things. If your baby cannot see, you may have to help her learn to roll over. As her head, neck, and shoulders get strong, you will notice your baby holding her head up and turning when she hears sounds. Now she can prepare for rolling over.

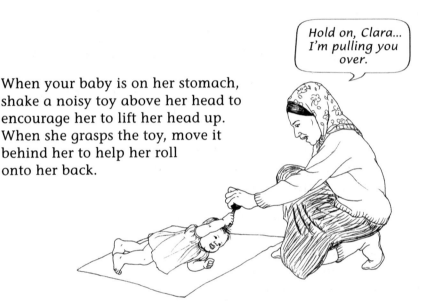

When your baby is on her stomach, shake a noisy toy above her head to encourage her to lift her head up. When she grasps the toy, move it behind her to help her roll onto her back.

Put your baby on her side with a cloth or pillow behind her. Shake a noisy toy in front of her. Then move the toy down to the floor. She will then turn her head and shoulders to follow it — and will roll onto her stomach.

4 TO 6 MONTHS OLD

When a baby gets a little older she can:
- smile in response to a familiar voice or sound
- explore her body to learn what it is like
- make sounds that are like words but do not make sense (babble)
- bring an object in her hand to her mouth
- move an object from one hand to the other
- reach for toys she hears, feels, or sees
- roll over from her back to her stomach, and from her stomach to her back
- get ready for sitting and crawling (for example, by trying to balance while sitting on someone's knee)

At about this age, a baby who is blind may begin to repeat movements over and over.

A child who is blind often repeats unusual movements over and over, like poking her eyes, flapping her hands, and rocking her body. No one knows for sure why this happens. It is probably because every baby needs to explore and play. If she does not know there are interesting things around her, a baby will play with the only thing she knows — her body.

You may notice these movements before your baby is 6 months old. These movements may harm her development if they keep her from paying attention to the people and things around her. As she grows up, other children may not want to play with her because her movements frighten them.

The activities in this chapter will give your baby many opportunities to learn new things.

Encourage your baby to explore and play, and she will probably make these movements less and less often.

▶ *To encourage your baby to reach for things and hold them*

Let her touch objects that have a different feel — for example, furry, smooth, or bumpy toys. After she begins playing with them, move them just out of her reach. Tap the objects on the floor, so she knows where they are.

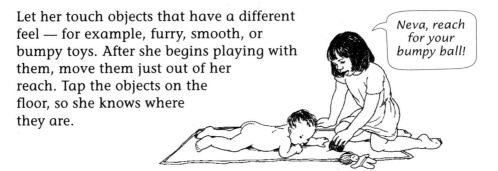

Neva, reach for your bumpy ball!

Shake a noisy object until she reaches for it. (At first you may need to gently push her elbow toward the object.) Then encourage her to shake it and move it from one hand to the other. This will help her learn where sounds come from and will also strengthen her arms.

Fasten objects to your baby's clothes or hands with a short string. If she drops a toy, guide her hand along the string until she reaches the top. This will encourage her to reach on her own and to learn that things she drops have not disappeared.

Keep a few objects in the same place so she can learn where to find them.

▶ To help your baby roll over

If you did the activity on page 39, you helped your baby roll over by pulling on a toy, or by putting something behind her back. Now she can learn to roll over with less help.

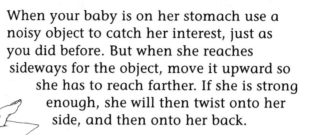

> Can you find the rattle, Simi?

When your baby is on her stomach use a noisy object to catch her interest, just as you did before. But when she reaches sideways for the object, move it upward so she has to reach farther. If she is strong enough, she will then twist onto her side, and then onto her back.

> Now where did the rattle go, Simi?

When your baby is on her back, encourage her to reach for a noisy object held to one side. Help her roll toward the noisy toy and onto her side or stomach.

▶ To prepare your baby for sitting up

If your baby is not yet sitting up by herself, these activities can help her get ready to sit.

> You're such a big girl now, Sekai. Sitting up all by yourself.

Hold your baby on your knees, facing you, and supporting her back.

> Listen to Tata and Pai. They are making balls with clay.

Sit behind your baby, giving her some support with your body.

Hold your baby loosely on your knees. Slowly lift one knee so she leans a little to one side. Then bend the other knee. She will learn to shift her body to balance herself.

▶ To help your baby prepare for crawling

To crawl, a baby needs strong arms and shoulders. She must also be able to balance while shifting her weight from side to side. These activities can help.

Place your baby on her hands and knees over a roll or cloth. The roll should be big enough to give her some support, but small enough that she has to bear some of her own weight. Slowly rock her forward and backward, and from side to side.

Place your baby over your leg or a roll of cloth. Encourage her to reach for a toy on one side, while her arms and knees on the other side take some of her weight. Repeat on the other side.

▶ *To help your baby enjoy moving and feel safer moving on her own*

You can help your baby enjoy moving by letting her move in many different ways. Keep talking to her as you do these activities. This will help her feel less afraid when doing something new.
For example:

Rock her back and forth in a large cloth or hammock.

Play a game where you and another person pass the baby back and forth between you.

Make up body movements to do together. Bend her legs and move them back and forth. Help her bring her hands together across the center of her body and back again. Bring her hands together and clap them. Use the same words each time to name what you do.

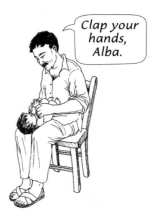

Strap your baby on your back and run or jump.

Chapter 6

Communication

Communication happens whenever:
- one person sends a message, and
- another person receives the message and responds.

A baby begins to communicate at birth, long before he learns to talk. Before a child can have a conversation with other people, he needs to learn many simple communication skills, like:

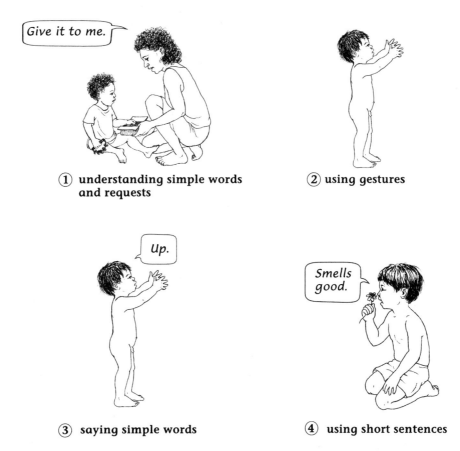

Give it to me.

① understanding simple words and requests

② using gestures

Up.

③ saying simple words

Smells good.

④ using short sentences

All these communication skills help a child feel close to his family. Later, these skills will help him learn to play with other children.

How vision problems affect communication

A young baby can send messages about what he thinks or feels by moving his body (like turning his head), by making sounds (like crying), and by changing the look on his face (like frowning). Family members learn to understand what their baby's messages mean and they respond.

You must be hungry.

Ali's such a quiet baby. Maybe he doesn't like to play.

All babies want to play. But this baby needs help to begin.

A baby who cannot see well may seem too quiet. He may send fewer messages because he may be trying to understand the sounds around him. His family can help him communicate by sending him messages in ways he can understand and by learning to understand the different messages he sends.

Parents must learn to notice the different kinds of messages their babies send. A baby who can see, for example, uses eye contact to show he is paying attention. But a blind baby may move his hands or body to send the same message. Or he may get quiet so he can pay attention to what is happening around him.

Parents must also send different kinds of messages back to their babies. It is easy to forget that a baby cannot see his parents' looks or smiles, and that they must send messages to him through touch and sound.

When I smile, I wish he'd smile back.

If she tickles her baby, he may smile back.

Talking to your child is very important

A child who cannot see well has a harder time than other children learning what words mean. This is because he often cannot see what is being talked about. And yet, learning to listen to others and to talk are especially important for a blind child because these skills help him understand the world he does not see.

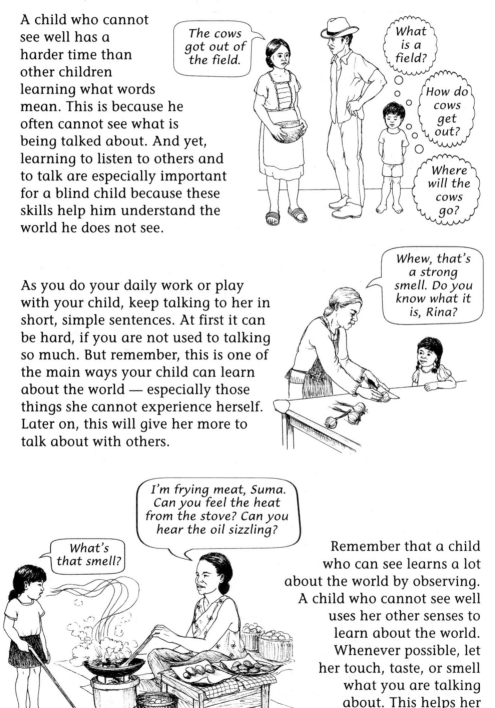

The cows got out of the field.

What is a field?

How do cows get out?

Where will the cows go?

As you do your daily work or play with your child, keep talking to her in short, simple sentences. At first it can be hard, if you are not used to talking so much. But remember, this is one of the main ways your child can learn about the world — especially those things she cannot experience herself. Later on, this will give her more to talk about with others.

Whew, that's a strong smell. Do you know what it is, Rina?

I'm frying meat, Suma. Can you feel the heat from the stove? Can you hear the oil sizzling?

What's that smell?

Remember that a child who can see learns a lot about the world by observing. A child who cannot see well uses her other senses to learn about the world. Whenever possible, let her touch, taste, or smell what you are talking about. This helps her begin to understand what the words mean.

ACTIVITIES

The activities below are divided into 2 sections:
- activities to use before your baby can talk, and
- more activities to use when your child begins talking.

If your child can see a little, be sure to adapt these activities to make the best use of his remaining sight (see Chapter 4).

Communicating before your child can talk

TAKING TURNS

Taking turns with your baby means (1) sending him a message or responding to messages he is sending you, and (2) trying to keep the give-and-take between you going.

Every time you take turns with your baby something different might happen. But here are some general guidelines that may help make taking turns work well:

1. To begin, let your baby know you are near and ready to play.

2. Let your baby take his turn first, so that he gives you a clue about what he wants to do. But if you have to wait a long time, go ahead and begin yourself.

3. When your baby responds in any way, consider that as his turn and respond to it. This way he knows you noticed his action and liked it. If he does not respond, try helping him with a 'prompt,' like a touch on his arm, to remind him it is his turn. It may also help to use activities that involve give-and-take, like rolling a ball back and forth between you.

> Do you want to play more, Juan?

4. When you take a turn, try to take the same amount of time as your baby took for his turn.

5. Allow your baby to stop whenever he wants. Most games of taking turns last only a minute or two because babies can pay attention only for a short time.

▶ *To encourage your baby to take turns*

Taking turns helps your baby learn that he can affect what others do by sending messages to them. This makes him more interested in the world and more eager to communicate. Taking turns also helps him learn important communication skills, like how to begin a 'conversation,' how to pay attention, and how to respond to his family's messages.

1. Marie lets her nephew Rene know she is near and ready to play by talking softly with him and then gently touching his arm.

2. When Rene responds to her touch by reaching out to explore her face, she responds to let him know he has done something important.

3. Marie waits for Rene to finish and then takes her turn, touching his nose with her finger.

4. She then waits for him to respond, and so on.

Preparing to talk

▶ *To help your child send messages with his body (gestures)*

Try playing games that
use gestures.

Where's your mouth?

This child is
learning that
pointing sends
a message.

Explain what different gestures mean.

*Don't just cry. If
you want to be
picked up, Barasa,
raise your arms
like this.*

*Good going,
Barasa, that's it!*

▶*To prepare your child for learning to talk*

Talk about any work or activities
you are doing and how you are
doing them.

*I'm washing the
floor, Kam San. You
can hear the water
splash when it hits
the floor.*

Here is another example:

Tobar's brother is using words to describe a game that Tobar likes to play.

Talk about things you do and about everyday objects.

If you use the words for body parts and common objects over and over in your everyday activities, your child will learn what the words mean before he can say them.

A child who has difficulty seeing cannot see how other people express their feelings, like fear or joy. He needs help understanding what feelings are. Encourage him to feel your face and his own face to learn how feelings are shown there.

Talk about feelings and emotions that you or your child experience.

When your child begins to talk

▶ *To help your child communicate with words*

A young child does not know enough
words to say everything he wants to say.
So he will often use a sound or word — or
several words — to say many things. Do
not tell your child that he said something
wrong. Instead, help his language grow
by filling in the words he did not say.

Wait for your child to ask for something rather than giving it to him first.

Ask questions that require more than 'yes' or 'no' answers.

Let your child take the lead when you are talking. Talk about what he wants to talk about.

When your child's message is unclear, let him know. Sometimes, no matter how hard you try, you cannot understand what your child is trying to tell you.

You might try asking him:

If you still cannot understand what he is trying to tell you, let him know.

Common problems when learning to talk

Children who can see get ideas for communicating from watching people talk. A child who cannot see well misses this and may learn to talk later than a child who can see. So, when learning to talk, a child who cannot see well often:

- repeats what others say rather than speaking his own thoughts
- uses words like 'he,' 'she,' 'it,' and 'you' (pronouns) incorrectly
- does not turn toward the person speaking
- asks a lot of questions

If your child is having some of these problems, here are some activities that may help.

▶ To help your child speak his own thoughts

It is natural for young children to repeat what others say. In fact, a young child should be encouraged to repeat words because this helps him learn to speak. But a child who cannot see well often continues repeating words for a long time, rather than learning to say what he is thinking. This happens because:

- your child may want to keep talking with you but not know enough words to tell you this.
- he may not understand your words, since he cannot see what you are talking about.
- he may repeat the words to try to understand what they mean.

If your child repeats what you say, let him know you heard him, and then expand on what he said. This shows your child that you are listening to him. It also shows him some other ways to respond.

Papa's going now, Rashid.

Papa's going now, Rashid.

Rashid, are you upset? Are you saying you don't want me to go?

Try to understand what your child is trying to say when he repeats your words. Often it helps to look for feelings and ideas he may want to talk about but does not know how to say.

This is a pineapple. Feel how rough the outside is. When we cut it open, the inside is almost smooth and very sweet.

Give your child many opportunities in the community to learn about the world and to touch the things you talk about. This will help him learn more words so he will need to repeat things less often. It will also show other people how they can help your child.

Do you want some soup?

If you are hungry, Noah, say "Yes, I want soup."

Do you want some soup?

As your child gets older, let him know that repeating what others say is not sending the right message.

▶ To help your child learn to use pronouns

Pronouns are words like 'he,' 'she,' 'you,' or 'it'. These words can refer to many different people or things. All children have some difficulty learning to use these words correctly. But children who cannot see well have more difficulty because they cannot see who or what is being talked about, or if the person talking is a man or a woman. It often takes an extra year or two for children who cannot see well to use pronouns correctly.

Use pronouns when talking to your child, even if he is not using them correctly. But make sure he knows you are talking to him. You can say his name first or touch him gently to get his attention.

Pedro, Juan and I want to play a game with you. Can you play with us?

Play games that teach parts of the body. When your child knows the parts of his body, help him identify the same parts on other people.

I have a mouth too. Can you find my mouth?

Where's your mouth?

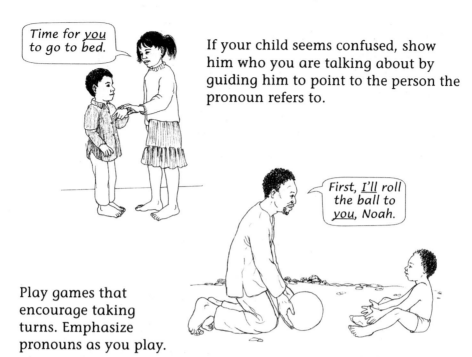

If your child seems confused, show him who you are talking about by guiding him to point to the person the pronoun refers to.

Play games that encourage taking turns. Emphasize pronouns as you play.

If your child is using pronouns incorrectly because he is repeating other people's words, try the suggestions in the previous section.

▶ To help your child face the person who is speaking

Because they do not see other people talking, children who are blind do not know that they should face the person they are talking with.

Encourage your child to turn toward other people when he is talking to them.

At first, you can gently turn his head toward you as you speak.

When he is older, teach him to face you as you speak.

▶ *To help your child ask fewer questions*

Most children go through a time in which they ask a lot of questions. But blind children often ask questions for a much longer time. This may be because:
- they cannot see what is happening around them.
- they do not know enough words to carry on a conversation.
- they want contact with another person.
- they are so often asked questions by adults.

If your child is asking so many questions that it is hard for you to answer them all, or if these questions seem to keep him from learning other ways of talking, he needs your help.

Look for the feelings that may be behind the child's questions.

What is Papa doing? What are they playing? When will they stop?

Sandeep, you'd like to play too, wouldn't you? Why not ask Papa, "Can I play, too?"

Describe new experiences before your child has them. This way he does not need to ask questions to find out what is going on.

Do you hear the loud noises? Men with big trucks are working on the road. Later, we can go and visit them.

Listen to how you talk to your child. Are you asking him a lot of questions? If so, try turning some of your questions into statements. For example, instead of asking "Do you want to go to bed?" say:

It's time for bed now.

Chapter 7

Thinking Skills

A child develops thinking skills by having many opportunities to play with the people and objects around him. Any activity that helps a child learn gives him new ways to think about the world. This chapter gives some ideas for activities that can help a child develop thinking skills. Most children who can see begin to learn thinking skills at about the following ages:

Between 6 and 9 months, a baby learns that objects still exist — even when he no longer sees, touches, hears or smells them. For example, if he drops a cup, he knows it has not disappeared but is now lying on the ground.

At about 9 months, a baby begins to copy what others do (imitation).

Between 9 and 12 months, a baby learns that he can make things happen. For example, he learns that if he hits a cup with a spoon, it makes noise. He also begins to solve simple problems.

At about 1 year, a baby can match 2 objects that are alike. Later, he will learn to sort and count objects.

A child who cannot see well can also learn these skills. With some help, he will learn them only 3 to 6 months later than a child who can see.

ACTIVITIES

If your child can see a little, be sure to adapt these activities to make the best use of his remaining sight (see Chapter 4).

Understanding objects

A baby knows that an object (or person) exists when it can be seen, touched, heard, smelled, or tasted. But if the object drops out of sight or no longer makes a sound, a baby thinks the object has disappeared.

A baby who cannot see well has more difficulty learning that these objects still exist than babies who can see. This is because he has less information about objects. For example, he may not be able to see that the object is still there when it stops making a sound.

▶ *To help your child understand that objects still exist when they cannot be seen, heard, felt, tasted, or smelled*

Tie strings onto toys and then onto chairs, tables, and your child's clothes or hands (see page 41).

Put seeds or small stones into a round gourd or ball so it makes a sound as it rolls. Then encourage your child to roll the ball back and forth between you. The sound will help him learn that the object still exists even after it leaves his hands.

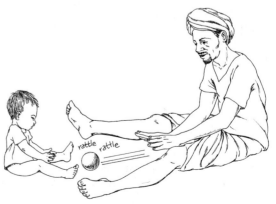

Tie a piece of string to a favorite toy. Show your baby the toy and string and then place the toy out of his reach. Encourage him to pull the string to get the toy. Remember, since strings can be a hazard for small children, watch him to make sure he does not wrap the string around his neck.

Do you hear your rattle, Rashid? Pull the string some more!

Show your child how to drop an object into a box and then shut the lid. Then show him how to open the lid and reach in to find the object again.

Juan, where's the rattle?

There it is!

Doing the same things others do (imitation)

Children who can see learn a lot by watching others and trying to do (imitate) what they do. Children who cannot see well, however, must learn to pay attention to sounds and other clues to know what people are doing.

▶ *To encourage your child to imitate others*

Imitate him. When your child makes a noise, make the same noise back.

Do something that makes a sound and encourage him to repeat what you do.

Oh, listen! The boxes fell down.

Can you push the boxes down, Noah?

When he gets older, encourage him to dress up and pretend he is someone else.

Here's Papa's hat. Now you be Papa.

Understanding why things happen (cause and effect)

When a young baby plays with toys, he does not know what will happen. But slowly he learns that by doing certain things — like banging a toy on the floor — he can make other things happen — like a loud noise. This is an important lesson for a baby, because he is learning that he can have an effect on the world around him. He also learns that he has some control over what happens. This makes him more curious about how things work.

▶ *To help your baby learn about cause and effect*

Place noisy toys across the area where he sleeps or plays. Make sure the toys are close enough so he will accidentally hit or kick them. Soon he will learn to hit and kick them on purpose.

That was a tall stack, Kontie!

Make a stack of small boxes or cans that your baby can knock down. As he gets older, he can learn to make the stack himself. Encourage him to see how high he can make the stack before pushing it over, and to notice the different sounds each box or can makes.

Encourage him to put things inside a box and then toss them out.

Solving problems

Your child has already learned something about solving problems. For example, if he cries when he wants something, he has learned that crying can get him what he wants. But by crying, he is asking someone else to solve a problem. He also needs to learn that he can solve many problems himself.

▶ *To help your baby learn how to solve problems*

Where's Luis?

There he is.

Put a cloth over his face. He may pull it off right away. But if he does not, pull it off yourself and then put the cloth on his face again.

Play hide-and-seek with your child's toys. Shake a noisy toy and then hide it under a cloth. See if he can pull the cloth off to find it. Next, try turning a bowl or a pan upside down and putting it over the toy. See if he can figure out how to turn the bowl over.

What's under the bowl?

Give your child a box filled with different sized objects and let him play with them. Then cut a hole in the lid of the box, but make the hole smaller than some of the objects. Put the lid on the box and encourage your child to take all the objects out. See if he can figure out how to take off the lid to get the biggest objects out.

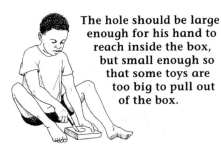

The hole should be large enough for his hand to reach inside the box, but small enough so that some toys are too big to pull out of the box.

The toy is too big to get out, isn't it?

What can we do?

Matching and sorting objects

Every child needs to learn how objects are similar to and different from each other. Matching and sorting objects helps teach a child to pay attention to important similarities and differences.

▶ To help your child learn how to match objects

Put 2 different objects — like a spoon and a pan — in front of your child and let him explore them. Then give him a third object that is like one of the first 2 objects. Ask him to find the 2 objects that are shaped the same.

Javier, there's something on the table just like this. Can you give it to me?

Ask your child to match objects that are the same size or color, or that make the same sound, or have the same feel.

If you find the big balls, Noah, we can play with them.

Cut a hole in a box that is the same shape as a simple toy. Then ask your child to find the same shape to put in the box.

▶ *To help your child learn how to sort objects*

Make a hole in a box and then ask your child to find all the toys that are small enough to go through the hole into the box.

All the small toys can go in the box. But some toys are too big.

Let's put the seeds in one pile and the stones in another.

Make a game of putting similar objects together in a pile.

Make a game of comparing objects.

Let's find the shortest stick. It will be good for making pictures in the sand.

Make a shape puzzle. Cut out shapes — like circles and squares — from a piece of strong cardboard. Help your child fit them back into the correct places. When he can do this, try harder shapes, like triangles and stars.

Counting

▶ *To help your child learn to count*

Throughout the day, look for ways
to teach your child to count.

Let's count the spoons you have. Are there enough for everyone?

Let's count the buttons: 1, 2, 3...

1, 2, 3...

Good, Pedro! You found the big balls. Let's count them: 1, 2...

When your child is
matching and sorting
objects, you can also
teach him to count.

Make a simple counting frame. Your child can slide beads or rings
from one side to the other to count, add, and subtract.

When your child becomes more skilled with
numbers, he can learn to use the methods
in your community that rely on touch, like
counting stones or using an abacus.

Increasing your child's thinking skills

As your child develops, he must learn to use his skills to form more complete ideas about the world around him. You can help by providing him with many different opportunities to learn about his world.

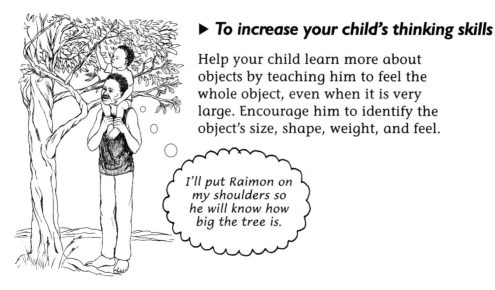

▶ To increase your child's thinking skills

Help your child learn more about objects by teaching him to feel the whole object, even when it is very large. Encourage him to identify the object's size, shape, weight, and feel.

I'll put Raimon on my shoulders so he will know how big the tree is.

If your child can see a little, ask him to describe objects to you or to draw them. This way you will know if he sees well enough to understand what the object really looks like. If he has not seen the object correctly, explain what it is like.

What a nice dog. Can you tell me what he looks like?

Help your child learn about all the different parts of an activity. For example, take your child with you to explain all the things you must do to prepare a meal.

Help your child learn how objects can change. For example, in the cooking example above, the child can also learn how the vegetables and eggs change and feel different after cooking.

Help your child connect one experience with another. For example:

Chapter 8
Teaching Everyday Activities

Your child is young now, but someday he will be an adult. A child who is blind or cannot see well can grow up to be a capable, contributing member of your family and community. Like other children, he must learn how to:

- take care of himself
- help with the family's work
- be independent
- be well-behaved

Taking care of himself

Daily living skills include eating, dressing, using the toilet, and keeping clean. A child who cannot see well needs to learn all these skills so that he can take care of himself. As he grows up, if he can take care of himself it will be much easier for him to go to school and earn a living.

It's so much easier for me to feed and dress Ayoka. It's going to take such a long time to teach her those things. I don't have time.

Yes, I know it seems hard now, but think of the time you'll save later. If Ayoka can dress herself, you'll have more time to do all the other things you have to do every morning.

My mother, Fola, is almost blind. Maybe she can tell you some things that would make it easier.

And think of how proud you'll be when Ayoka can dress herself. You don't want to be dressing her still when she is a big girl.

Helping with your family's work

While he will need some help at first, a child who is blind or cannot see well can learn to help with the family's work, just as all children can. Give him small tasks at first, so he can feel successful. Then, as he develops more skills, give him more difficult tasks. This makes less work for you and shows your child he is an important part of the family. This will build his confidence and give him hope for the future.

A young child can begin to learn about farming by planting seeds and caring for the growing plants.

Later, the child can go with his father or mother to the fields and help with the planting. His feet can follow the rows made by the plow.

Help her understand the whole process of a task. For example, explain about a meal — where food comes from, how it is prepared, where dishes are kept, and how they are cleaned after a meal.

Carmencita, I'll teach you to wash the dishes we just used.

Being independent

Being independent means that a child has a chance to do things by himself, without help from other people. Sometimes, because families worry about their blind child's well-being, they protect him too much. Then, when he is older, he will not know how to do things by himself.

It is better to teach your child how to do new things safely than stop him from trying new things.

Being well-behaved

Children who are blind or cannot see well need firm, loving discipline just like any other child does. But sometimes people feel so sorry for a blind child that they do not set limits on his behavior, and they let him do things they would not allow other children to do. Try to make the same rules for all your children.

Luis, that's Julia's food. Please eat the food on your plate.

Tuan Jai, keep your mouth closed when you chew your food.

Teach her the same manners that other children learn. Although a blind child will have some different eating habits than other children — like touching her food to know what and where it is — she should learn the eating habits used in her community. Then she can eat with other people without her family feeling shame.

ACTIVITIES

If your child can see a little, be sure to adapt these activities to best use her remaining sight (see Chapter 4).

Eating

Blind children can learn eating skills at the same time as children who can see. Expect your child to do what other children her age in your community can do. These ages differ from community to community. But many children learn eating skills at about these times:

Birth to 4 months: A baby sucks and swallows. She also learns to open her mouth when she is about to be fed.

6 months or older: Along with breast milk, she begins to eat soft, mashed foods, like cereal or rice. She may begin drinking from a cup.

6 to 12 months: She begins feeding herself small bits of food with her hands. She should still breastfeed whenever she wants it.

9 months to 1 year: She begins to eat mashed foods and to use some eating tools, like a spoon.

1 to 3 years: She learns to better use eating tools and a cup.

3 years: She can eat most adult foods.

A child who cannot see well will learn to feed herself more quickly if she eats about the same time every day, in the same place, and with other people. This helps her learn that eating is done in a certain way. She will also learn the names of foods more quickly if everyone in the family uses the same name for the same food.

▶ *To prepare your child to eat by herself*

Before your child begins feeding herself, you can help her prepare to learn these skills.

When nursing your baby, give her a sign, like touching her cheek, to let her know you are about to feed her. As she feeds, place her hand on your breast. This helps her learn where the milk comes from.

Marisol, open your mouth. Here comes the rice.

When you start feeding your baby soft foods, tell her when you will be putting food in her mouth. Let her touch the bowl and keep her hand on yours as you bring the food to her mouth. Describe what she is eating and how it tastes, and encourage her to touch and smell the food. If she spits out the food, keep trying. She needs to get used to eating in other ways than sucking on a breast.

Encourage your baby to try different kinds of food. When she can eat mashed foods, feed her the same foods that adults eat. Then she is more likely to want these foods as she gets older. If she does not like foods with different textures, keep trying. Eating different foods will help her learn to swallow well.

Eloho, here are some yams...mmm Mama's favorite!

Let your child touch the food before you feed her.

If your baby cannot hold her head up, hold her in your lap and support her head with your arm. To help strengthen her neck muscles, see page 37.

▶ *To help your child learn to eat by herself*

When she is learning to drink from a cup, first let her feel the cup and the liquid inside. Then let her hold the cup and smell the liquid as you guide it to her mouth. Encourage her to take a sip of liquid. Finally, help her set the cup back down in the same place.

Where's your mouth? The food goes straight to your mouth, Meliza.

Your child will eat best if she is sitting up straight.

When your child begins to pick up foods with her hands, let her feel and smell the food. At first she may need a lot of help putting the food in her mouth, but slowly she will be able to do more herself.

Help your child learn to use the eating tools — spoons, or chopsticks, or fingers — your community uses. Teach her how to hold the tool, how to pick up the food, and how to bring the food to her mouth. Slowly give less and less help. Sit behind her as you guide her hand. Be patient. Your child will be messy at first. It usually takes a year or more for a child to become good at these skills.

Your beans are on the right, and the rice is on the left — just like always.

Even after your child begins using eating tools, let her touch the food so she knows what the foods are and where they are in her bowl. It also helps to put her food and drinking cup in the same place at each meal.

Let your child eat with the rest of the family so she learns that eating is a social time. Encourage everyone to include her in what is happening.

Uh-oh...Anita, that noise was your brother spilling his milk.

Help your child learn to bite off pieces of food with her front teeth and chew with her back teeth. Show her what chewing is by putting her hand on your jaw as you chew. If she does not follow your example, gently move her lower jaw up and down to show her how chewing feels.

Feel how my mouth moves, Arti? That's how I chew my food.

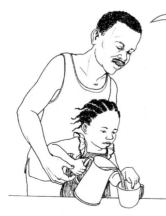

When the water touches your finger, Irene, stop pouring.

When your child can hold a jug or pitcher, help her learn to pour her own water. By putting a finger in the top of her cup, she will know when it is full. (Try this yourself with your eyes closed.)

Dressing

Children learn dressing skills at different ages, depending on local customs. Many children, however, learn dressing skills at about these ages:

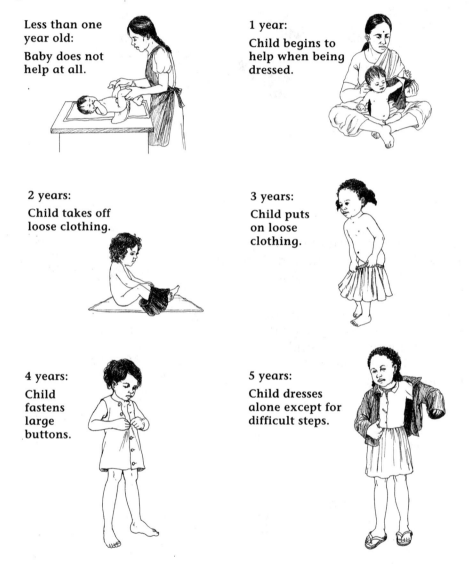

Less than one year old:

Baby does not help at all.

1 year:

Child begins to help when being dressed.

2 years:

Child takes off loose clothing.

3 years:

Child puts on loose clothing.

4 years:

Child fastens large buttons.

5 years:

Child dresses alone except for difficult steps.

A blind child will learn to dress herself more quickly if she dresses in the same place every day. It also helps if family members use the same word for each kind of clothing, and if they give the same instructions in the same order each time. It is best to teach dressing skills when your child needs them — for example, when taking clothes off for a bath or putting clothes on before going outside. This helps her understand why she takes her clothes off and puts them on.

▶ *To prepare your child to dress and undress by herself*

Let your child touch what she is about to put on. This helps her get to know the feel of the clothing and how it is shaped before she puts it on. Describe the clothing and what color it is.

Meena, here's your red shirt.

As you dress your child, tell her the name of each piece of clothing and the part of the body it goes on.

Now I'm putting your red shirt over your head.

Rosa, hold out your right arm so I can put on the sleeve of your yellow shirt.

Ask your child to help you as you dress her. This will help her learn that she plays a part in getting dressed.

▶ *To help your child learn to undress and dress herself*

Mark the back of your child's clothes (with a knot, a small piece of material, or a safety pin) so that she can tell the difference between front and back. Also mark one of her shoes, so that she can tell the difference between the right shoe and the left.

It is easier for a child to take her clothes off than to put them on. So first teach your child to take her clothes off.

To help your child learn to put on pants, first help her find the front of her pants. Then help her put them on.

To help your child put on a shirt, explain that there are 3 holes and that the largest one is for her head. Then:

Help her gather up the shirt so she can get her head through the large hole...

Yena, first find the big hole for your head.

...and put each arm into a sleeve and pull the shirt down.

Then put your arms through the smaller holes.

Help your child learn to unbutton buttons. It may be easier to try this on adult clothes first, since the buttons are bigger. When she can unbutton, teach her to button.

Xiang Yi, hold the button in one hand, turn it on its side, and push it through the hole in the shirt.

Teach your child to put her clothes away in the same place each time. That way she can find them easily and will need less help.

After I wash the clothes, Olivia, I hang them to dry in the sun.

Teach your child how clothes are washed and dried.

Using the toilet or latrine (toilet training)

'Toilet training' means helping a child stay clean and dry. A child is toilet trained when:

- she knows when she needs to use the toilet and has learned to wait so she does not dirty her clothing or the floor.
- she goes to the toilet by herself, asks for help cleaning herself, dresses herself, and gets rid of the waste (if necessary).

The age when children become toilet trained varies from child to child. It also varies from place to place, depending on local customs. With help, many children can stay dry by age 2 or 2½. Blind children may take a little longer to become toilet trained than children who see.

When your child can stay dry for about 2 hours, she can begin to recognize the feeling of needing to go to the toilet. This is the time to begin toilet training.

▶ *To prepare your child to learn toilet skills*

When changing her diaper (nappy), always use the same words to describe the difference between wet and dry diapers. Let her feel the diapers so she can tell the difference.

Take your child to the toilet with you and describe what is happening. Use the same words each time. Make sure everyone in the family uses the same words.

Use the same route to go to the latrine, so your child will learn the way.

▶ *To help your child learn to use the toilet on her own*

Notice when your child typically wets her diapers and take her to the toilet just before this time. Do this throughout the day, at the times she is most likely to be wet (for example, after eating, before sleeping, and before going to bed at night).

Teach your child to tell you when she needs to use the toilet. She can use a certain word or sign to tell you.

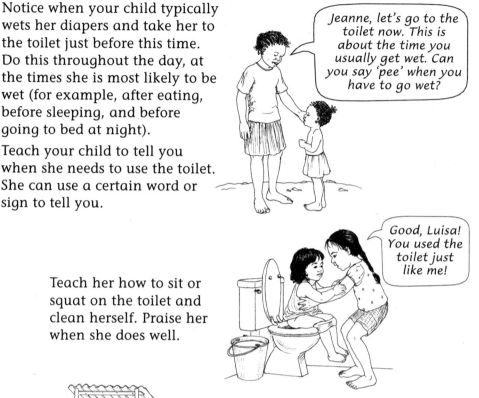

Teach her how to sit or squat on the toilet and clean herself. Praise her when she does well.

Stay with your child while she uses the toilet until she is not afraid to be alone. Show her how to hold onto the rail and put both feet on the ground, so she will not be afraid of falling in.

If your child wets herself before getting to the toilet, take her to the toilet and change her clothes there. This way she will learn to connect having dry clothes with sitting on the toilet.

Keeping clean

A blind child needs to learn to wash her hands, take a bath, brush her teeth, and comb her hair, just as all children do.

▶ To teach your child how to keep clean

Help her learn about keeping clean and why it is important. For example, as you wash and dry your hands, describe what you are doing and the parts of the body you use. Let her feel your movements, the water, and the towel.

> I'm washing my hands to clean off the dirt.

> I don't want to get dirt on my food.

Help your child do the activity herself. Work from behind and help her by putting your hands over hers. Use the same words and the same motions each time you help her. Give less and less help as she learns to do it by herself.

> Rub your hands together, Ramona, to get the dirt off. After you use the soap, rinse your hands with water.

> Sika, if you brush your teeth after you eat and before you go to bed each day, your teeth will stay healthy.

Do these activities at about the same time each day. This will help your child remember to do it.

> If I put the towel back here, I can find it again next time.

Keep the things your child needs in the same place, and teach her to return them to this place when she is done. Make a special mark on things that only she uses, like a toothbrush.

Chapter 9

Safety

When children first begin to crawl and walk, we often pay a lot of attention to their safety. As a child learns to move around, he also learns to avoid things that might harm him. Children who can see can avoid many dangers. But you need to be extra careful if a child cannot see well.

There are many things you can do to make your home safer and to teach your child about hazards. And by working together with people in your community, you can make your village or neighborhood safer for your child and others — often these changes will benefit many people.

▶ To help your child move about the house safely

Cover sharp corners on furniture, cupboards, and objects. Remember, not all dangerous corners and edges are at floor level.

Try to keep furniture and objects in the same place, both inside and outside your home. Tell your child if you move something.

▶ To help your child identify dangers

Warn your child about hazards such as fires, hot pans, and wet floors. Place a marker, like a mat, to help him know how close he can come.

▶ To help your child move safely when the ground is not flat

Make the floor as even as you can by fixing holes and bumps.

Put railings next to stairs inside and outside your home. Put a gate across the stairway until he can crawl or walk up and down safely.

These are a few examples. You will find your own safety problems and solutions in your home. For more information about helping your child move about safely, see Chapter 10 on "Movement."

We were worried that we wouldn't think of all the dangers our child might find. Then our older children suggested that they close their eyes and walk slowly around our house so they could find safety problems. Afterward we all talked about ways we could make our home safer.

▶ To make the area outside your home more safe

Cover all open wells, ditches, and holes. Show your child where these are and explain what and why they are there.

These boards will cover the well behind our house.

This fence keeps the chickens from getting out, Manuel. It's between the house and the big tree.

Make fences safe to touch and high enough that a child will not trip over them. Show him where the fences are and explain what they are for.

Put a barrier between your house and a busy street until your child learns to stay away from traffic. A sign can also remind people to drive slowly.

If you know other parents with blind children you can work on safety together. Try meeting with your neighbors to discuss how the community can be made safer for all children. (See Chapter 15 for information about parents groups.)

Chapter 10

Movement

A young baby has little control over how he moves. But slowly, as he grows, he gains control first of one part of his body, then another:

First, he gains control of his head and body (trunk)...

...next he develops arm and some hand control...

...and finally, leg control.

Children learn to move because they are interested in something, like a toy, and want to reach it. A child who cannot see well will need more encouragement to move because he may not know there is an interesting world to explore.

For a child who does not see well, movement may also be frightening. Help your child get used to movement by encouraging him to move from the day he is born. If your baby is less than 6 months old or does not move much, first read Chapter 5 on "Activities for the Young Baby."

When your child can control his head and sit with help, he is ready to begin the activities in this chapter. These activities will help your child learn to:

- sit by himself and crawl
- stand, walk, and use a cane
- have strong, flexible hands and arms
- feel fine details and shapes with his fingers

For information on keeping your child safe, see Chapter 9 on "Safety." For information about safety when walking in new places, see page 112. For information on ways to encourage play between your child and other children, see page 129.

ACTIVITIES

If your child can see a little, be sure to adapt these activities to best use his remaining sight (see Chapter 4).

▶ *To help your child sit by himself*

Place your child in a sitting position with his legs apart and his arms in front to support himself. Show him some toys and then put them in different places, like between his legs, and on the right and left sides of his body. As he moves to find the toys, he will use and develop his balance.

> Here's your spoon, Noi — and your rattle.

> Where did the spoon and rattle go? Can you find them?

▶ *To help your child learn to crawl*

When your child can lie on his stomach and push his upper body up with his arms straight, he is ready to start learning to crawl. The activities in this section can help him learn to move his upper and lower body separately, to put weight on his arms and legs, and to shift his weight from side to side. All these skills are important for learning to crawl and should be done in the order shown here.

1. When your child is lying on his stomach, put some toys at his side near his waist. Then help him push up on one hand and reach for a toy with the other hand.

2. Place your child over one of your legs so that his arms are straight and his knees are bent. To help him bear weight on his arms and legs, and to shift his weight from side to side, rock your leg from side to side while pushing down gently on his shoulders and lower back.

3. Place your child sideways across your leg. Have some toys within reach in front of him on the right and left sides. Encourage him to reach for a toy, first with one arm, then the other.

Try to find your toy, Ahmed.

Here's your favorite shaker, Diego. Can you come and get it?

4. If your child drags his stomach as he starts to crawl, support his stomach with your hands or with a towel. As he moves toward a toy, pull the towel up slightly on one side, then the other, so that he learns to shift his weight from side to side. As he becomes more able, give him less support.

Come get your rattle, Kontie.

5. Once your child can stay in a crawl position on his hands and knees without help, encourage him to reach for a toy. Try to keep him moving forward so he does not sit back on his bottom.

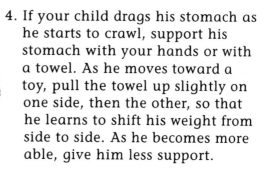

6. Once your child can crawl easily, encourage him to crawl up stairs. Place his hands on the first step and move up with him. Then help him turn around and come down the stairs by sitting on his bottom.

Just one more step, Alfredo. Then we'll play with your cup and box!

As soon as your child is crawling, you will need to make sure that the places where he crawls are clean and safe for him.

▶ *To help your child learn to stand*

Let's bounce up and down, Natife.

Hold him in a standing position on your lap. Bounce him up and down a little so he gets used to feeling where his feet are. Also move him gently from side to side so he learns to shift his weight.

Sit on the ground with your legs apart. Encourage your child to hold onto your body and pull himself into a kneeling position, and then to stand up.

Keep pulling, Anil. There you go!

Put toys he likes on a chair or table and encourage him to pull himself up to get them. Or put your hands on his hips to help him up.

Up you go, Viku!

I'm holding you, Manuel. You can sit down.

To help your child lower himself from a standing position to a sitting position, support his bottom as he lowers himself to the floor.

▶ *To help your child learn to walk*

Encourage your child to walk
back and forth, holding onto a
piece of furniture. This will also
help him learn where different
things are in the house.

*Come to me, Thet
Nay, for a big hug.*

*Let's walk to
the table,
Pablo.
Everyone's
ready for
supper.*

When his balance is
better, hold one of
his hands and walk
with him.

Let him start walking alone by pushing a
simple walker, chair, or box. Put some
weight in the box or chair so he has to
push harder and so it does not move
too fast.

**Be patient. It takes a long
time for a child to feel
safe walking without
holding on to anything.**

Once your child is walking, be sure to think about possible dangers in
your home and the area around it, and how to make walking safer.

▶ *To help your child learn to walk up and down stairs*

To help your child walk
up stairs, encourage him
to stand up and hold onto
the rail and move one
step at a time. Later,
teach him how to go
down the stairs too.

Hold the rail,
Fernando, so
you won't
hurt yourself.

▶ *To help your child use his arms for guidance*

As your child gets older, he can learn to use his arms to guide
and protect himself while walking.

At home, he can use the back of his hand to
follow a wall, the edge of a table, or other
objects.

**This boy's hand is
touching the wall
for guidance.**

In other places he can hold one hand in front of
his face, with his palm facing away from his body.
This hand protects his face and head. He should
hold his other hand about waist high, to protect
the rest of his body.

When he falls, teach him to protect himself by
putting out his hands and bending his knees as he
falls. This will keep him from hurting his head.

Accidents will happen just as they do
to children who can see. But it is
important to let your child do things
for himself, to learn to be
independent.

▶ *To help your child learn to use a stick (cane)*

A child can start learning to use a stick whenever he seems ready, usually when he is 3 or 4 years old. Using a stick can help a child feel more comfortable when walking in new places.

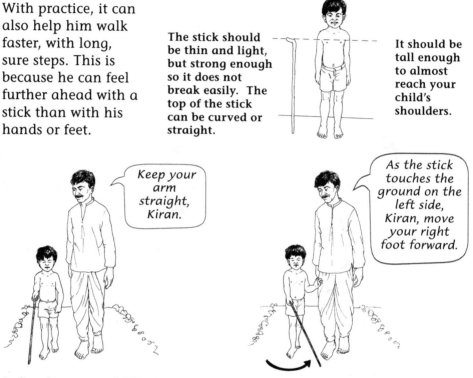

With practice, it can also help him walk faster, with long, sure steps. This is because he can feel further ahead with a stick than with his hands or feet.

The stick should be thin and light, but strong enough so it does not break easily. The top of the stick can be curved or straight.

It should be tall enough to almost reach your child's shoulders.

Keep your arm straight, Kiran.

At first, have your child lightly touch the ground in front of him with the stick as he walks. Stop before he gets tired. 5 to 10 minutes is enough at first.

As the stick touches the ground on the left side, Kiran, move your right foot forward.

As he gets used to using the stick, teach him to move it from side to side, lightly touching the ground. The width of the swing should be a little more than the width of his shoulders.

Your child can also use a stick to help him go up and down stairs and curbs:

YES

Teach him to hold the stick like this to feel the height and position of each step.

NO

Do not hold the stick like this! The step may make the stick stop suddenly and hit him in the stomach.

▶ *To help your child learn many kinds of movement*

When your child can walk easily and is steady on his feet, let him move around in open places where he will not bump into things. When he feels sure of himself, he can learn all the different movements of a child his age:

pushing

pulling

sliding

balancing

swinging

climbing

dancing

Hand and finger skills

All children develop hand and finger skills, but these skills are harder to learn for children who cannot see. A child who cannot see well must learn to control his fingers, hands and arms because he depends so much on them to give him information about the world. These skills are also important when he learns to read Braille (see page 139).

Children who cannot see well may not be as active as other children. Encourage your child to participate in the everyday activities that will help him develop:

- strength and flexibility in his hands and fingers
- the ability to feel small and fine details and shapes with his fingers

as a young child

older and
at school

beginning to
learn a trade

▶ *To help your child develop strength and flexibility in his hands and fingers*

Give your child tasks or make up games in which he uses his finger muscles — for example, rolling balls of mud or clay, kneading bread dough, shelling peas, or squeezing oranges.

Give your child tasks or make up games in which he breaks or tears things — like grass, leaves, corn husks, or shells — into little pieces.

Now we have enough stuffing for the pillow, Pierre.

Encourage your child to do things that require turning his hand, like wringing the water out of wet clothes, opening jars with screw-on lids, or turning the radio off and on.

Encourage your child to scribble and draw. Drawing in wet sand or mud lets him feel the shapes that he has drawn.

Teach your child games or skills in which he must use his fingers separately, like putting shoelaces through the holes of his shoes or tying knots.

Teach your child crafts, like weaving, knitting, or crocheting, that require skillful use of his hands.

Activities like pushing toys through a hole in a box (see page 66), eating with the fingers or with eating tools (see page 76), and using buttons (see page 81) are all good for developing strength and flexibility.

▶ *To help your child develop the ability to feel fine details and shapes with his fingers*

Let your child crawl on different surfaces, like wood floors, rugs, wet and dry grass, mud, and sand.

Isaac, the floor is smooth and cold. But the rug feels warmer, doesn't it?

Can you find your winter shirt, Domingo? It feels thicker than your summer shirt.

Encourage your child to find his own clothing by the feel of the material.

Good, Sonu! You can find the stones and dirt in the rice as well as I can.

Ask your child to help with chores in which he must feel the differences between small things.

Can you follow the string with your fingers, Francisco?

That shape is called a circle.

Glue string or yarn in different patterns on a piece of paper or cloth. Then let your child trace the lines with his fingertips.

Chapter 11
Helping Your Child Know Where She Is
(Orientation)

Rani is a little blind girl, born in a village in India. Rani's grandmother Baka is blind too, and has been able to show Jeevan and Aruna, Rani's parents, ways to teach Rani. By the time Rani was 2 years old she had learned to feel her way along the walls and furniture. She moved slowly, carefully exploring each crack, bump, and crevice with her fingers. Now Rani's family wants to teach her to walk in the house without holding on to things.

Today, Baka is explaining to Jeevan and Aruna how she learns to get from place to place. "When I want to go from the front door to my favorite chair, I walk 8 steps. That takes me past the table. Then I make a quarter-turn to the left, and I walk another 4 steps. Then I reach out my hand and make sure the chair is there, because I remember one time somebody moved the chair, and I sat down on air!" Baka laughs as she remembers.

But Baka's story is not funny. It is important for us to understand how hard it is for a blind child to learn to get around. For Rani to learn to walk without holding on, she will have to remember every detail — how many steps to walk and how far to turn. Rani's family will have to be patient because it will take Rani a lot of effort and practice.

How a child learns to know where she is

A child who can see uses her eyes to know where she is and where objects are. A child who cannot see well needs to know these things too, but she must learn to use her other senses. When she does, she will be able to move around her home and later become active in the community. To learn how to orient herself:

she must learn where her body is in relation to other objects

The door is right in front of me.

she must learn where objects are in relation to other objects

From the door, the woodpile is just ahead, on the right.

You can help your child learn orientation skills by: (1) teaching her about her body and the way it can move, (2) helping her develop her senses, which give important information about her surroundings, and (3) thinking about things around your home or neighborhood that she can use as landmarks.

BODY AWARENESS

A child learns the names of the parts of her body by watching and imitating other people. A child who cannot see well will learn the names of different parts of her body when you teach her to use her sense of hearing and touch. For activities that help a young baby learn about her body and develop her senses, see Chapter 5, "Activities for the Young Baby." Many of these activities are also good for older children.

▶ To help your child learn the names of different parts of her body

Make up games in which you ask your child to do things with different parts of her body and with your body. To give you some ideas, here are a few examples:

Ask your child to touch part of her body and then touch the same part on your body.

Can you touch my mouth, Majoya?

Ask your child to roll over on the floor and name each part of her body as it touches the floor. This is a good group game too.

Now your stomach is touching the floor. Roll over again, so your back touches the floor.

Mei Mei, your arms help you carry things.

Wrap a cloth around different parts of your child's body and ask her to take it off. Explain the name for each part of the body and what it does.

Raise your arm and wave bye-bye, Alba.

Encourage your child to nod her head, kick, and to wave — and name the body part she uses.

▶ To help your child learn about the relationship between her body and other objects

Your child needs to learn ideas like "in front of you" and "to your left" to know where things are. Here are some ways to help her learn.

Try getting her attention with a noisy toy. Tell her where the toy is — in **front**, **behind**, or on the **right** or **left** side. Then move the toy, tell her where it is, and see if she can find it herself.

Now the rattle is behind you. Can you find it?

If she has trouble knowing right from left, tie a ribbon or bracelet on one of her wrists.

Roibita, let's see how many stones you can pick up with your right hand. Then put them on your left knee.

After she can tell the right side of her body from the left side, hand her different objects and ask her to put them on one side or the other. Gradually make the games harder.

I've hidden the ball underneath the table. Let's see if you can find it.

Make up a game in which she gets **underneath** things (like a table or a bed), **on top of** things (like a bed), **in between** or **around** things (like a table and chairs), **through** things (like a door) and **inside** things (like a big box). Explain what each movement is.

First go forward, then to the left to get your ball...

Make up different games in which she must move her body forward, backward, or sideways in order to find a toy. Explain what each movement is. If you make up a song that names each movement, she will remember them better.

Sight

Children who can see a little can use their sight to help orient themselves, especially if you help them.

If your child can see light, give her directions using a light source as the starting point.

When you see the light from the door, the table where we eat is on your left.

My bed is next to the light.

If your child can see light, leave a light on so she can orient herself when she comes into a room.

Put a light where the height of the floor changes or next to something your child needs to notice to move about safely.

Here's the yellow ribbon. That means it's Juana's door.

If your child can see bright colors, put different colored cloths, tape, paint, or objects on a door and in different places outside. When she sees the color, she will know where she is.

Hearing

Hearing is especially important for a child who cannot see well because it gives her information about things that are not close by. Sounds help a blind child know what something is, where it is, and how far away it is. As often as you can, bring your child close enough to touch the object that is making the sound.

▶ *To help your child identify and locate sounds*

Play a game where your child names everyday sounds at home and in the community — like a door closing, a chair scraping against the floor, or a sewing machine.

What's the sound you just heard, Juanita?

Play a guessing game in which your child identifies family members and animals by the sounds they usually make.

Who's making that chopping sound, Sylvie?

Mama

Azlina, that sounds like your cousins playing music. Can you go and find them?

You can also ask your child to move toward the sound.

Have your child listen to the sound of your footsteps as you walk toward her and then away from her. See if she can tell which way you are walking. Or clap your hands as you move closer and then farther away. Then stop and ask her to find you.

Teach your child to listen for how the sound of her footsteps (or her cane) changes when she is near a house or wall, and when there is open space. With practice, she can learn to tell how near things are by these sounds. These skills will help her when she is walking by herself in the community.

Touch and feeling

To know where she is, your child needs to learn to notice the shape, weight, and texture of objects around her. She also needs to learn to pay attention to the feel of the ground under her feet and the way temperature can change as she moves from place to place.

▶ To help your child develop her sense of touch

Throughout the day, encourage your child to touch objects of different sizes, weights, and textures. Ask her to describe what she feels. You can then place different objects and textures around the house to help your child know where she is.

Fiam, feel this blanket. What does it feel like?

Soft, just like my dress.

Encourage your child to walk barefoot on different kinds of ground — for example, on dirt, grass, and gravel — so she can learn how each one feels. If she wears shoes, she can then put them on and see how the ground feels different. When she is walking outside, this information will help her know where she is or help her stay on a path.

What does the ground feel like, Olanike?

Teach your child how to use her feet to feel for differences in height, like at the edge of a road or sidewalk.

Encourage your child to notice when the temperature changes as she moves from place to place.

When Ai-Ling feels the air get cool, she knows she is almost at the door to her home.

Clara knows that she should feel the sun on her back when she comes home from the market in the afternoon.

Smell

Smells, like sounds, can give information about things close by or at a distance. To understand how to use smells, your child needs to learn to identify different smells and where they come from. You can use your everyday tasks to help your child learn about smells in the community.

▶ *To help improve your child's sense of smell*

When you are walking, explain the different smells around you — for example, from food, flowers, animals, garbage. If at all possible, bring your child close enough to touch the object that she smells.

The next time you walk together, see if she can name the smells herself...

...and ask her to walk toward the smell or away from it.

Throughout the day, point out different foods and household things that have strong smells. See if your child can identify them.

Other orientation skills

To become independent, a child needs to learn to walk in new places and to follow directions. These activities may be difficult for your child to learn and may frighten her at first. It may also be difficult for you to give directions that she can follow. You can be a better teacher for your child if you:

- try the activities with another adult first. Blindfold each other and practice all the steps. Talk about how you can make the instructions clearer.
- then try teaching a child who can see. Blindfold the child and lead her through the same steps that you tried with an adult. Pay close attention to her reactions so you can find ways to reassure and encourage her.

▶ To help your child follow directions

When your child is comfortable walking by herself, teach her how to make turns.

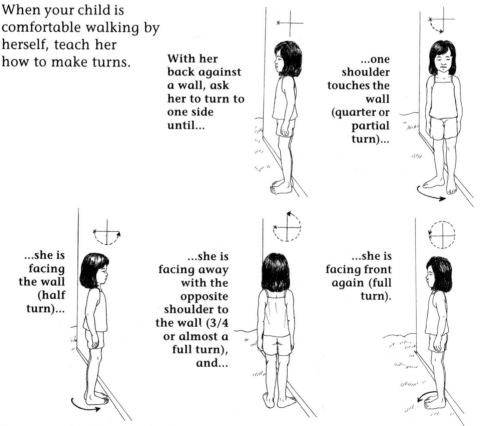

With her back against a wall, ask her to turn to one side until...

...one shoulder touches the wall (quarter or partial turn)...

...she is facing the wall (half turn)...

...she is facing away with the opposite shoulder to the wall (3/4 or almost a full turn), and...

...she is facing front again (full turn).

Encourage her to pay attention to how her feet move as she does this. Gradually she can move away from the wall and practice on her own. Remember to be patient. Your child will need a lot of practice before she can make turns on her own.

▶ *To help your child learn to walk in a new place*

These activities will help your child learn about:

- landmarks (any object, sound, or smell that is always in the same place).
- clues (objects, sounds, and smells that give good information but are not always in the same place).

These activities should be done in the order they are described here:

> Good, Celia. You got around that rock safely.

1. First, play a game in an area your child knows well. Tell her you have put some things in her path, and see if she can get past them without slipping or falling. This will help her feel more confident about trying to walk in new areas.

2. Then let her hold on to one of your fingers and walk a step behind you through a new place.

> This gate is a good landmark, Celia.

> The chickens are a clue to where you are. But remember, chickens move around so they won't always be here.

3. As you walk, help her identify landmarks and clues. Be sure to teach her about any dangerous landmarks, like a river or a street.

We're just about to go through the gate now, Celia. You can tell because the path gets rocky.

4. When she feels comfortable in that area, walk through it again — only this time walk backward, in front of her, and talk to her while you are walking.

That's right, Celia! You have a good memory.

5. Finally, walk behind her while she describes what is around her.

   Be patient. It takes a long time for a child to feel comfortable walking alone in a new place.

Here are the rocks. The gate comes next.

6. When your child is confident, give her directions starting at a known landmark and explain where to go from there. Do this for very short distances at first, then gradually increase the distance.

You start from this doorway to take Papa his lunch, Marina. You'll go under the big tree, where it gets cool. When you step into the sun again, take a quarter turn to the right. There you'll find the path to the field.

How the community can help

People in the community can help make it easier for your child to find her way.

Community members can learn to give directions that will help her find things on her own. Chapter 13 talks about the special help community members can give to a child who cannot see well.

People can also put landmarks in places that will help your child find her way or know where to turn. Each village or neighborhood is different, so you and your community will have to decide what things are right for your child. Here are two examples of landmarks that can be community projects to help a child who cannot see well:

Putting posts or other markings where paths cross can help your child find her way.

Putting a guide rope or rail can help your child find her way.

Chapter 12

Preventing Sexual Abuse

As children become more independent, they meet more people and relate to them in many different ways. Just as they must learn to move around the house and community safely, they must also learn about personal safety. This chapter is about protecting children from sexual abuse.

It might seem strange to find material about sexual abuse in a book like this. Sadly, children with disabilities like blindness can be more at risk for sexual abuse than children who can see, so it is important to discuss.

Keep our children safe

Nobody has the right to use a child for sex.

- *Not a relative (child or adult)*
- *Not a family friend*
- *Not a neighbor*
- *Not a stranger*
- *Not a teacher*
- *Not a caregiver*

Parents need to talk about sexual abuse with each other, and with our children. Talking about it is the first step in stopping it. Not talking about it only protects abusers.

Yet it is hard to talk about sexual abuse. In many places:

- people rarely talk about sex.
- people do not want to believe that sexual abuse happens to very young children, so they do not think or talk about it.
- rules or customs say who should talk to children about sex, what should be said, and when such conversations should happen.

> **Every child should be able to be safe from sexual abuse. Keeping children safe from sexual abuse should be every adult's responsibility.**

Some facts about sexual abuse

Sexual abuse is any direct or indirect sexual contact between an adult (or older youth) and a younger child. Sexual abuse can happen to any child. It happens in all communities, and in rich and poor families. It happens most often to girls but also to boys.

There are many different kinds of sexual abuse. Some of the most common are:

Abuse that involves touching a child:

- kissing or hugging a child in a sexual way
- sexual intercourse
- oral sex (mouth to penis or mouth to vagina)
- touching a child's sexual parts or asking a child to touch an adult's sexual parts

Abuse that does not involve touching a child:

- using sexual language to shock a child or make her sexually excited
- making a child hear or watch sex between other people
- making a child pose for pictures
- forcing a child to become a prostitute

Most sexual abuse starts when children are older than 5 years, but it can happen to younger children too. Most abused children are abused by someone they know, like a family member or neighbor — not by a stranger. Often the abuse goes on for a long time, sometimes for years.

We do not know exactly how common sexual abuse is, since children often do not tell anyone. But it is possible that as many as 1 of every 4 children in the world are sexually abused.

Sexual abuse can be physical — like intercourse, or touching or kissing sexual parts. But it doesn't have to be physical touch — it can be sexual talk too.

Sexual abuse has lasting effects

Even though talking about sexual abuse is hard, it is very important to make sure that you, or someone you trust, talk to your child. Explaining sexual abuse to children in a way they can understand will not make them more worried. It will not hurt them. It will make them safer.

Sangeeta was 4 years old when she was abused by her 14-year old brother. She went to her parents and in her childish way told them that her brother had hurt her. At first, Sangeeta's parents thought that she had bruised herself. Sangeeta did not know the right words to use, but she kept trying to explain.

Finally, when her parents understood what had happened, they did their best to cover up the incident. Sangeeta was not allowed to talk about it. Her parents "solved the problem" by sending her brother to a boarding school. For her parents, the matter was closed.

As Sangeeta grew up, her brother's abuse had lasting effects on her. She was afraid of men and she felt it was her fault that her brother had been sent away. When he came home for holidays, she could not talk to him. Sangeeta was convinced that she could never get married. She felt shame and was afraid of having "pain" again, she said. She also felt little hope for the future and had little faith in herself or her abilities.

When she was 16, Sangeeta began talking to her aunt who was a health worker about her childhood abuse. As she shared her feelings and fears, she began to gain confidence. Finally, with her aunt's support, she was able to share her feelings with her brother, who asked for her forgiveness. She is happier now, but she is still not able to talk to her parents about her feelings.

Sangeeta was fortunate because she was able to find someone to talk with about her feelings. Sometimes victims of abuse pretend that nothing happened. Sometimes they do not remember what happened until they begin talking about why they feel so afraid or unhappy. When adults who were abused as children cannot talk about their own feelings, they often cannot talk to their own children about how to protect themselves against abuse either.

Why is my child at risk for sexual abuse?

Sometimes adults feel like they have the right to use a child sexually. Sometimes older children do not realize they are doing something bad.

All children are at risk for sexual abuse because they trust adults and older children, and depend on them for care. This makes it difficult to say 'no' to them. Very young children also have less developed thinking skills and do not know what is acceptable adult behavior.

Children with disabilities are especially at risk for sexual abuse because they must often depend on other people for care even more than children who do not have disabilities. In addition, children who are blind or cannot see well:

- may have less developed communication skills. This can make it difficult for them to understand what you say about their safety. It can also make it harder for you to understand them if they try to tell you about abuse.
- may have less information about their bodies, and the differences between boys' and girls' bodies, than children who can see.
- miss important information, like a look on someone's face, that can sometimes help children learn safe social behavior.

Not all people who abuse children sexually use physical force. They can use:

- persuasion and sweet talk
- threats and bullying
- tempting treats

The result of the abuse is still violent and damaging to a child.

I want Mishiri to be safe, and I worry about her. But I have no idea how to teach her to protect herself from people who want to hurt her or use her. My mother never talked to me about this.

I know what you mean. I feel uncomfortable, myself. But I know it is really important.

Let's practice talking about it with each other. Then we will feel better prepared to talk to our children.

Preventing sexual abuse

▶ To help your child learn about his or her body

A child about 18 months old can begin to learn the names of parts of the body.

When your child is between 3 and 5 years old, teach about the genitals and other private parts of the body and about the differences between boys' and girls' bodies.

Teaching can happen naturally, for example, while your child is bathing.

Children who are blind or have vision problems may need extra help learning about the parts of the body. See pages 102 and 103 for activities that will help. Using realistic dolls may also be helpful to teach about body parts.

▶ To help your child understand about his or her private body parts

Explain that some parts of the body are more private than others. Explain that people should not touch your child's genitals or private parts, and your child should not touch the private parts of others, even if asked to.

Also, remember to explain that not all sexual abuse involves touch.

No one else should touch your private parts. If someone asks you to touch places that are private, that is wrong.

Also if someone is talking to you about private things or asking you to watch private things, that is wrong, too.

▶ To help your child learn to say 'no'

Help your child trust his feelings and encourage him to talk to you about what he feels.

Ask your child to tell you or another adult right away if someone asks him to do anything he feels uncomfortable doing.

> Have you ever wanted to stay away from some children because you felt they were going to harm you?

> Yes.

> When you have those feelings about the way someone is treating you, come talk to me about it.

Help your child practice saying 'no.' First, try making up situations in which a child may want to say 'no.'

> Norma was on her way to school and a boy came along and pushed her down. How did Norma feel? What could she do about it?

Later, talk about saying 'no' and where your child can get help.

> You can say 'no' to other children who want to touch your body. Yell 'no' over and over and fight back until they stop.

> Some people don't respect the rules about no touching. Where could you go for help if I am at work? How about your Aunt Rose? Or Lisa's mother? Who else?

▶ *To help your child understand that he or she does not always have to obey bigger people*

Teach your child that she should shout 'no, no,' scream, bite and struggle if an adult or older child tries to assault her.

▶ To help your child understand about secrets

Talk about secrets that are OK and not OK.

> *If we don't tell Jean that Grandma is coming for her birthday, it is an OK kind of secret.*

> *But we don't keep secrets about the private parts of our bodies. Be sure to tell me if anyone wants to touch your private parts.*

Explain to your child that if someone threatens her to keep her from talking about something, she must tell you. An abuser may say things like *This is our secret. If you tell anyone, I will kill you or kill the person you told. And I will tell everyone about the bad things you did.* Reassure your child that nothing bad will happen if she talks to you. A child needs to know that an abuser makes these threats because he is doing something bad, not the child.

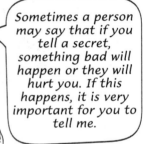

> *Sometimes a person may say that if you tell a secret, something bad will happen or they will hurt you. If this happens, it is very important for you to tell me.*

▶ Respect your child's growing need for privacy while bathing or dressing

A blind child may find it hard to understand the idea of private body parts because he or she needs help in so many everyday activities. But you can encourage your child to tell you when he or she does not want help.

> *Don't come in.*

> *OK, Lora, I'll wait outside.*

How can I know if my child has been abused?

When young children are abused, they may be afraid to tell you because the abuser warns the child not to say anything or because the child fears she did something wrong. Or a child may lack the communication skills to say what happened.

Since children do not always tell about abuse, you need to watch for possible signs. The following signs are not **always** the result of abuse, but they should cause concern, especially if a child shows several.

Some physical signs include:

- unexplained pain, swelling, or bleeding of the mouth, genitals or around the anus area
- torn or bloody underwear
- difficulty passing urine or stool
- sexually transmitted infections (STIs)
- bruises
- headaches or stomach aches

Sexually abused children may:

- stop bathing, or wash themselves more often than usual
- play in a sexual way with other children or with toys
- know more about sex than other children their age

Children who have been victims of violence, including sexual abuse, may:

- seem very fearful, sensitive and watchful, or suddenly avoid or become afraid of certain people or places
- want to be with their parents all the time
- be secretive or prefer to be alone most of the time
- start acting in a younger, more baby-like way
- try to run away from home
- feel sad most of the time or show no feelings at all
- have difficulty sleeping because of bad dreams and fears of the dark

If you suspect abuse, try to stay calm. To get more information, try asking your child questions about how she is feeling. It may help to set up play situations that encourage your child to show you what has happened or what she knows. Listen carefully and make sure your child knows you believe her.

If your child has been sexually abused

If your child has been sexually abused, you can help if you:

- believe what she says. Children rarely make up stories about sexual abuse.
- praise her for telling you. Children need to know that they have done the right thing by talking about the abuse.
- reassure her that the abuse is not her fault and that you are not angry with her.
- protect her safety. Try to prevent future contact between the child and her abuser. If this is not possible, make sure you or someone who knows what happened is always with your child when the abuser is present.
- treat physical health problems from the abuse. Try to get your child tested for sexually transmitted infections, even if she does not have any signs. Some sexually transmitted infections do not have any signs, or they do not come until a child is older.

As a parent, you also need help. Parents feel many emotions including disbelief, anger, and sadness when they learn their child has been abused. Parents may blame each other for what happened to their child. It can help to talk about these feelings with someone you trust. Be patient with yourself. It may take a long time for these feelings to change.

To make all children in the community safer

Programs in schools and community meetings can educate the entire community about sexual abuse. Acting out short plays or skits sometime makes it easier for people to discuss abuse as a group.

Plan workshops for parents to help them learn ways of communicating with very young children about sexual abuse.

Hold meetings to decide how your community can respond to cases of sexual abuse. Some communities have suggested public shaming by gathering in front of houses of known abusers.

Chapter 13

Becoming Part of the Community

Children who cannot see well are part of the community, just like all children. But too often children who cannot see are kept at home. They seldom play outside, or walk, or help with their family's work. These children have little chance to get to know other people, and other people do not get to know them. People may even think that blind children cannot learn how to do things. When children who cannot see go out into the community, people may be unsure how to talk to them, or how to act.

As parents, you can do a lot to help your child become an active member of the community. Take your child with you as much as possible — when you collect water, or gather wood, or when you go to the market, or to school, religious services, and community meetings and events. Along the way, describe what you see and encourage her to listen to sounds, and to touch and smell things. Introduce her to the people and animals you meet, and teach her how to greet people.

How community members can help

Community members can learn that a child who cannot see well is just as active as other children. But she also needs special help getting to know people and finding her way about. People may feel uncomfortable with your child until you explain how to act.

▶ To help community members interact with your child

Encourage them to speak to your child whenever they see her. Ask them to introduce themselves and to call your child by name, so she knows they are talking to her. Explain that they should speak directly to her, rather than asking other people about her.

Marta, it's Maria and Rafael. How nice to see you.

Where are you going, Marta?

Encourage people to help your child find what she is looking for. Community members can learn to give directions (see pages 111 to 113) that will help her find things on her own.

Which way is the market?

Go straight ahead until the path gets rocky. Then take a quarter turn to the left.

Encourage people to answer your child's questions and to explain things to her. As members of the community get to know your child, they will begin to realize that she can do more than they would ever have thought possible!

I'm frying cakes, Suma. They're in a pan next to you. Can you hear them cooking?

What's that smell?

How other children can help

Children can be cruel to a child who cannot see well. They may be cruel by teasing, laughing, imitating, or even hurting her. But more often they are cruel simply by leaving her out of their games or activities.

▶ *To help children understand what it is like to be blind*

Often children act in a cruel way because they fear what they do not understand. When they gain more understanding, children can become another child's helper or friend. Here are some games that may help children understand blindness:

Game: Blurred vision

Children can find out what it is like not to see well if they:

put on somebody's strong eyeglasses or a pair of scratched sun glasses

cover their eyes with a piece of thin paper or other material that allows them to see just a little

To see these letters I have to get this close. And they're still hard to see!

Then have the children try to see something with small details, like the pattern on a leaf or the letters on a tin can. Ask the children what it feels like to try to see these things. How close do they have to get to see well?

Game: Guiding a blind child

Have children get into pairs. Tie a cloth around one child's eyes, so she cannot see at all. Let the other child be her guide. The guide takes the 'blind' person for a walk, lets her feel different things, and helps her move safely.

After the game, encourage the children to talk about these questions:

- How did it feel not to be able to see?
- Were you afraid?
- What did your guide do that was helpful or not helpful?
- What might he have done better?
- Did you trust your guide?

Game: Feel a friend

Tie a cloth around one child's eyes so she cannot see at all. Then let her try to recognize her friends by feeling them. Or she can try to recognize different objects. Then talk together about what it was like not to be able to see.

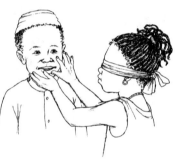

Game: What's that smell?

Tie cloths around the eyes of a group of children, so they cannot see at all. Then put in front of each child something with a strong smell like a peeled orange, tea leaves, coffee beans, a banana, or local plants. See if the children can recognize these things by their smell.

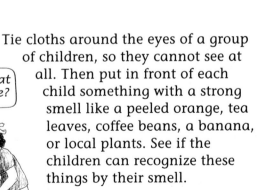

After the children play these games, explain to them that because blind people cannot see, their sense of touch, smell, and taste usually gets very strong.

▶ To help children include a child who cannot see well in their games

Often children do not realize that a child who cannot see well can play with them if they make small changes in their games. For example:

When she could hear the ball, Rina could join in the game.

Here are some more suggestions for including a child who cannot see well:

A bag filled with beans or rice can be used instead of a ball in a game of toss. The bag will make a sound when it is thrown and when it lands. Or try playing 'catch' by rolling a ball along the ground. A child can hear the ball as it rolls and catch it.

If a child can see bright colors, use brightly colored cloth for the bag.

A child who cannot see well can join a game of tag if the other children clap their hands or whistle as they run, or have something tied on each of them that makes noise.

A child who cannot see well can learn to jump rope if there is a bell tied to the rope.

A young child can use a can for a drum, a rattle made from a can with stones in it, or bottle caps strung on a wire to make different kinds of music (see page 185).

Drawing pictures in wet sand or mud helps a child feel what she draws.

A child who cannot see well can run races by using a rope tied between 2 trees, like this:

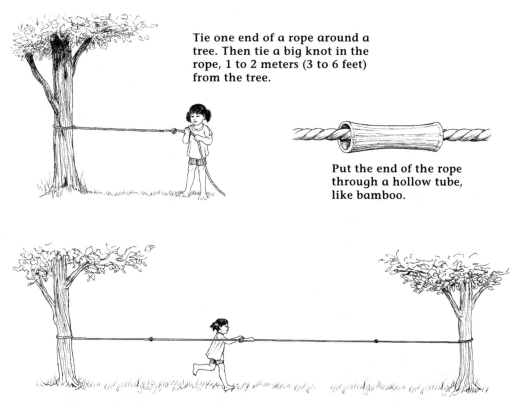

Tie one end of a rope around a tree. Then tie a big knot in the rope, 1 to 2 meters (3 to 6 feet) from the tree.

Put the end of the rope through a hollow tube, like bamboo.

Tie another big knot 1 to 2 meters from the second tree. Then tie the rope around the tree. Be sure the tube cannot go past the knots.

For more ideas, ask the children in your community. See who can come up with the most ideas of how to include a child who cannot see well in the games children play.

Community projects

Building a playground is an activity that can help children and community members learn to work together. There are some simple things that make play areas fun for all children. Then children who cannot see well will not feel left out. The ideas suggested here will be enjoyed by all the children in the community.

BUILDING A PLAYGROUND

To build a playground, it is best to use local, low-cost materials and simple construction. The playground will give children and parents a chance to try different playthings. Whatever works for their child, a family can later build at home, at no or low cost. For this reason, a playground made of tree limbs and poles, old tires, and other 'waste' materials is better than a fancy, expensive, metal playground built at high cost.

A Playground For All

Ribaralta is an isolated town in Bolivia. Because of bad roads, it takes 30 hours to drive from Ribaralta to the closest city. It is a poor town. There is no water system, and many of the people who live in Ribaralta do not have electricity. A group of parents of children with disabilities had begun meeting every 2 weeks. They discovered that they had become experts about their children's needs.

Because they had learned so much about disability, they wanted to educate the community about children with disabilities. They decided to build a 'playground for all children' that would bring disabled children and non-disabled children together through play.

The parents' original idea, which they thought would take 3 Sundays of work, became a much bigger project as people began to think of more ideas for the playground. They got businesses and farms to donate bricks, nails, wood, and trees. The finished playground included a fence, benches, trees, and playground equipment made from local wood and used tires.

Children enjoy crawling through well-cleaned old barrels or drums. Children who are blind will enjoy the echoes their voices can make inside the drums.

Try to include different kinds of swings. Build some swings low enough for small children to reach by themselves.

Children who cannot see well will be able to find and use the play equipment if it is painted with bright colors. Children who are blind will be able to find their way around if paths have edges, and if some play areas have grass and some have no grass.

Children love to make sounds by hitting or tapping things. Children who are blind will especially enjoy this kind of play.

Playground suggestions

- Involve as many people in the community as possible in building and maintaining the playground. The playground must be cleaned and repaired regularly, and this will require planning and organization.

- Keep the playground simple and build it from local, low-cost materials. This way, people can copy the ideas and build equipment for their child in their own homes.

- For poles that are put into the ground, use a kind of wood that does not rot quickly. Paint the part that will be underground with old motor oil, tar, or other insect- and fungus-resistant substances.

- Swings can be hung from ropes or chains. Ropes are cheaper but may rot or wear through quickly. Plastic or nylon rope will not rot in the rain but it will grow brittle and weak in the sun.

- Check the strength of poles and ropes frequently by having several heavy people pull on them at one time. Replace the ropes when they first start to weaken.

- Make sure that children are included in the playground design, construction, and maintenance. Much of the work can be done by children with adults to guide them.

Chapter 14

Getting Ready for Child-care and School

In some communities, there are places where young children are cared for while their families work. They are often called nursery schools, day-care centers, child-care centers, preschools, or creches.

A child who is blind or cannot see well can go to a child-care center with other children. And when your child is old enough, she should attend school like other children her age. In order to make these experiences fun and successful, you can:

- help your child prepare for child-care or school
- help the child-care center or school teacher prepare for your child

Helping your child prepare for child-care and school

▶ To learn to play with groups of children

At school, your child will be playing a lot with other children. Long before she goes to school, you can help her prepare by encouraging her to play with others, and by helping other children play with her.

If your child has experience playing with friends before she starts school, she will find it easier to make new friends once she is in school.

▶ *To learn what child-care or school is like*

If your child does not spend much time with older children, she may not understand what happens at child-care or school because hearing stories about school is how many children learn about it. A child who is blind or cannot see well may also be afraid to be away from her family for several hours. To help her understand about child-care or school:

Tell her some of the exciting things about child-care or school.

But I won't know anybody there. I'll be all by myself.

You will make new friends, and you will be hearing stories and having fun.

Ask an older child to "play school" with your child.

Now I'm the teacher. This is an "O."

▶ *To get to know the child-care or school building*

Your child will feel more comfortable on her first day of school if she has visited the school before and has learned how to get around on her own. Try to visit and meet the teacher when there are no other children present.

And this is where you'll be sitting, Cheng.

Let's try going from your seat to the door.

Helping the school get ready for your child

▶ *To help the teacher understand your child*

A teacher who has not worked with children who are blind or cannot see well may be unsure about how to teach your child. You know more about your child than anyone else, and there are many things that you can share with the teacher. Here are a few things you may want to talk about with the teacher:

- Tell the teacher about your child's skills and abilities.
- Show the teacher how to help your child move around the school.
- If your child can see a little, explain what she can see and how your child uses her sight.
- Remind the teacher that your child cannot see gestures or facial expressions, so instructions have to be spoken.
- Discuss any challenges your child has.
- Share information about blindness and how it affects a child's development.

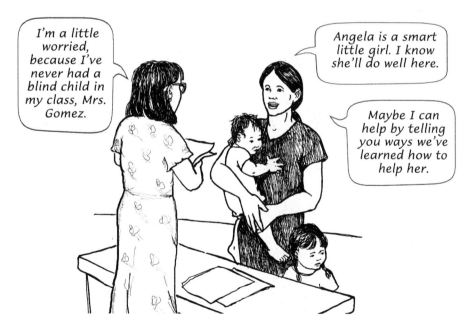

The section on how community members can help, starting on page 126, has suggestions the teacher might find useful too. You may especially want to share some of the ideas for helping children understand more about blindness and ways to include children who cannot see well in children's games.

▶ *To prepare the classroom for your child*

Talk to the teacher about the classroom, and see if there are simple ways to make the room safer and more comfortable for your child. You may want to:

- explain how a child who is blind can bump into things and how it helps to keep doors fully open or closed
- explain the importance of keeping things in the same place so that your child can move around with confidence
- decide if it will be better for your child to sit in the front of the room near the teacher

If your child can see the letters of the alphabet, the teacher should write on the blackboard in large thick letters and check often to see if your child can see them.

Preparing to read and write

If your child can see a little, try to find out if anything would help your child be able to see letters. If your child can see the letters of the alphabet, he may be able to read by:

wearing glasses

using a magnifying glass (a piece of glass that makes small letters look bigger)

reading large-print books in which the letters are bigger so they can be seen more easily

If your child has trouble keeping up with the reading at school, you can:

- ask someone to read books and lessons aloud to him.
- ask someone to read his books into a tape recorder, so he can listen to the books later.
- consider teaching him Braille (see page 139). This may be the best choice if your child's eyesight is likely to get worse.

Learning to read and write Braille

If your child cannot see letters or is blind, a specially trained teacher can teach him to read and write using a system called 'Braille'. Braille may look difficult, but that is only because it is new to you. Most children and adults can learn Braille easily.

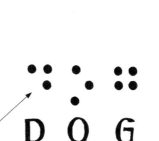

There may be special schools or classes for children who are blind, and teachers who will teach Braille to children.

To read Braille, a child runs his fingertips over patterns of bumpy dots that stand for letters of the alphabet. These 'letters' are put together to make words, like this.

D O G

To write Braille, a child can use different tools. These are the most common writing tools — a slate and stylus.

A child writes with a slate and stylus by pushing the tip of the stylus into heavy paper on the slate. The stylus pushes dots into the paper. He can then turn the paper over to read the raised dots with his fingers.

A child will be able to learn Braille more easily if he has strong, flexible fingers. For more information, see page 98.

School is important for all children

Because blind children often do not have the same opportunities as children who can see, school is very important for a blind child's future. Blind children can go to school and learn a lot, including skills they will need to earn a living.

In some places, children who are blind can go to special schools for the blind. Some local schools may have special programs for children who are blind. With some extra help, blind children can do well in classes with children who can see.

Chapter 15

Support for Parents and Caregivers

As a parent or caregiver of a young child who is blind, you need support and information that is useful for your family and your community. Although families and communities are different around the world, many of the challenges of taking care of a young child who is blind or cannot see well are the same, no matter where you live. This chapter talks about how many families in different places:

- feel when they learn their child is blind or cannot see well
- cope with the extra responsibility of having a blind child
- join together to support each other and to improve the lives of their blind children
- work as a group to get their community to support children with disabilities

As with the rest of this book, the information in this chapter is for you to adapt for your family and community.

When you first learn your child cannot see well

Learning that a child cannot see well or is blind can be very upsetting for parents and family. It is normal to feel upset by the news of your child's disability and to continue to feel different emotions in the months that follow. You and your family may feel:

- worry about what to do

  I don't know anything about blindness. What should I do for my child?

- denial (refusal to believe that your child will never see as well as other children)

  If I can just find the right treatment, maybe my child will be able to see.

- fears of what it means to be blind and fears about the future

  What will happen to my child? How will she get married or earn a living?

- guilt about what you might have done to cause the blindness

  If I had worked less during my pregnancy, this would never have happened.

- sadness, helplessness, or no feelings at all (depression)

  I feel so hopeless....

- anger at what has happened

  It's not fair that this happened to my family.

- loneliness

  No one else knows what this is like. No one can help.

- shame because your child is disabled

  What will our neighbors think?

As a parent, you may find it comforting to know that these strong emotions can help you cope, and at the same time can help you begin to take action to help your child. For example, denial may keep you from feeling overwhelmed by the sudden changes in your life. Some parents say that anger or frustration has given them energy to help their child and to reach out and help other families of children with disabilities.

Touli feels angry that this has happened, but I feel sad all the time.

You, your partner, and your family will probably feel some of these emotions and react to them in different ways. It is best to let each person feel the emotions in his or her own way, without judgment.

These emotions will slowly become less strong. Over time, you will begin to realize that your child has the same needs for love, affection, discipline, and learning as other children. And, like all children, she will give you much support, pleasure and joy. The fact that she cannot see well will become less important.

Look at how much joy her brother gets from playing with Delphine! How could I have ever thought she would be a burden to our family?

What if she can't keep up with the other children?

Many of these emotions will probably return at important times in your child's life, like when she starts school. The fact that they come back does not mean something is wrong. It just means that you are going through another period of adapting to your child and her disability. Usually the emotions will be less strong than the first time you had them.

Managing the stress of caregiving

All parents and caregivers need to find ways to manage stress. Parents and other family members work very hard caring for young children.

If one of the children cannot see well or is blind, then there is even more work.

Besides caring for the child, family members also need to be teachers, to help their child learn what other children naturally learn through sight.

At times it can be difficult to cope with this extra work. Here are some suggestions from families about different ways that have helped them manage:

BE REALISTIC

Try to be realistic about how much time you and others can spend working with your child.

Try adapting activities so they fit more easily into your daily life and take less time.

Whenever I make dinner, Pedro and I can talk about what he did that day. And he's learning to count by setting out plates for dinner.

Try breaking large tasks into smaller, easier tasks. This way you will see progress and not get discouraged.

I want Pradeep to learn to dress himself.

Why not teach him one thing first - like how to take off his shirt?

CARE FOR YOURSELF

Everyone needs time for themselves once in a while. But often parents do not take any breaks because they have so much work to do. If you get so tired that you do not feel well, then you cannot help your child.

To help yourself relax, take some slow, deep breaths. Try not to think about all the things you have to do, just for a while.

meditation

Many communities have developed beliefs and traditions that help calm the body and mind, as well as build inner strength. Practicing these traditions may help you take care of yourself.

tai-chi

TALK WITH YOUR FAMILY

Everyone in a family plays a role in a child's life. Each person caring for a child, especially one with special needs, may have different

ideas about the best way to raise and help that child. It is important to find time to talk together. This will help everyone understand how others feel. And if one of you is feeling tired or discouraged, the others may be able to help.

ASK OTHERS FOR HELP

You do not need to do all the activities with your child by yourself. Everyone in the family can help — so can friends and neighbors.

If you are feeling tired or discouraged, often just talking with another person can help. Try to find someone you can talk with often.

You look tired. Can I help?

Talk to a blind adult, a health worker or school teacher, or someone who teaches children who are blind. This will be especially helpful if your child does not seem to be learning new skills after several months.

It seems like Guddi should be walking by now.

Let me talk to Mrs. Patel, who teaches blind children in the city.

The power of parents working together

Working with other parents of children with disabilities can help in many ways. Working together can provide an opportunity to:

- share feelings and information
- give each other ideas about activities to help the children and the best ways to adapt activities for a particular child
- share ideas to help fit a child's activities into family and community life
- work together to make the community more friendly, safe, and supportive for children with disabilities

Sometimes I come to these meetings tired and discouraged. But the energy of others gives me strength.

I know. When I have a problem, I always feel better after talking about it here.

I was so relieved when the group helped me understand the real cause of Bayani's blindness.

If you know there are other parents like you, but there is no parents group in your area, you may decide that it is up to you to start one. Some of the strongest, most active parents groups began because of one person's idea. As a group, parents can work together to solve problems. Parents working together can do more than if they each work alone.

Our group sent someone to talk with the National Association for the Blind in the city. Now a field worker who knows about blindness comes to some of our meetings.

STARTING A GROUP

Find 2 or more parents who want to start a group. If you do not know other parents whose children cannot see well, you may want to include parents of children with other disabilities. A health worker may know of parents in nearby communities.

Plan when and where to meet. It helps to find a quiet place, like a school, health post, cooperative, or place of worship. At the first meeting, discuss why you are meeting and what you hope to do.

Probably one person will be the leader of the first few meetings. But it is important that no one person makes decisions for the group. Everyone should have a chance to talk, but try to keep the discussion focused on the main reasons for the meeting. After the first few meetings, take turns leading the group. Having more than one person lead each meeting will help shy members participate.

LEARNING TO SUPPORT EACH OTHER

Even when parents know each other well, it may take time to feel comfortable talking about feelings, experiences, and the challenges of raising a child with disabilities. These things take practice. Here are some suggestions for helping group members feel comfortable and trust one another:

Listen carefully to what others say, without judging it. Think about how you want others to listen to you, and then try to listen to them in the same way.

Try not to tell other people what to do. You can help others understand how they are feeling, and share your own experiences. But everyone must make their own decisions about the best way to care for their children.

Respect each person's privacy. Never tell others what the group talks about unless each person says that it is okay.

PLANNING FOR ACTION

When parents work together they can take action to solve many problems. Here are steps for taking action that other parents groups have found useful:

1. Choose a problem that most people in the group feel is important. Although many changes are probably needed, your group may be more effective if it works on one at a time. At first, pick a problem that your group has a good chance of solving quickly. Then, as the group learns how to work together, you can work on more complicated problems.

2. Decide how you want to solve the problem. List many ways the problem could be solved, and then pick the one that best uses your group's strengths and resources.

3. Make a plan. Members of the group will need to do different tasks to get the job done. Try to set a date when each task should be finished.

4. When you meet together, talk about how the work is going. Adjust your plan as needed if difficulties arise.

WORKING TOGETHER FOR CHANGE

Parents groups work on many kinds of projects. They may try to improve the economic conditions of families, the attitudes of communities, the government's laws and services for blind children — all as a way to help their children.

Most blind children come from poor families. To get more resources for their children, a parents group can:

- find ways to get funding for new projects to help children with disabilities
- help parents develop new job skills
- offer workshops on ways to teach and help children with disabilities
- develop groups and camps for the brothers and sisters of children with disabilities

These mothers learned how to sew clothing so they could earn more money, work closer to home, and spend more time with their children.

Parents groups can work to make the community more friendly and safe for all children with disabilities. Often, involving your neighbors in fixing safety problems in the community (see Chapter 9) is a good way to begin building solidarity with people with disabilities.

Many parents groups have worked to educate the rest of the community about disabilities. They use discussion groups, workshops, radio programs, newsletters, billboards, street theater, and posters to help others understand more about disabilities.

Other parents groups have worked on projects to help children with disabilities become more active members of the community. For example, your parents group can:

- organize sports events that include children with disabilities.
- build a playground for all children (see Chapter 13 "Becoming Part of the Community").
- start a child-care center where children with disabilities can be cared for together with other children (see Chapter 14 "Getting Ready for Child-Care and School").

Some parents groups have worked to improve government programs and laws for children with disabilities. Your group can:

- contact people in government, like the ministers of health and education. Tell them about services your community needs, or about laws needed to protect children with disabilities.
- get well-known people, like entertainers or athletes, to speak out in solidarity with children with disabilities.
- write letters, pass around petitions, or organize protests if government officials do not improve conditions for disabled children.
- educate and involve newspaper, radio, and TV reporters in your campaigns.

Parents groups have also worked to prevent blindness and other disabilities. For example, many children become blind because they do not eat enough foods with vitamin A (see Chapter 16 "Why Children Lose Their Vision and What We Can Do"). Your group may want to raise awareness about the causes of blindness, or grow vegetables that can prevent blindness.

Here is a story of how one parents group, Los Pipitos, is working to change the lives of children with disabilities.

Parents Are the Heart of Los Pipitos

In Nicaragua, there are more than 200,000 children with disabilities. Poverty is the most frequent cause. Eye problems and other disabilities often happen when children do not have enough to eat and live in crowded homes where infections spread easily.

Before 1987 there were few services for children with disabilities in Nicaragua. Then, 21 parents decided to form a group to "change the world." They called the group "Los Pipitos," which is a term of affection for children throughout Nicaragua. Los Pipitos now has more than 20 parents groups throughout the country. Together, these parents have become leaders in a national campaign to help children with disabilities.

We share our children's lives — their achievements and setbacks — and feel a deep sense of injustice when others reject them.

That is why parents and families are at the heart of Los Pipitos.

We reach out to other parents to bring them together, to share ideas, and to support each other.

Los Pipitos parents groups have:
- held workshops for parents on raising children with disabilities
- trained health workers about how to know the extent of a child's disability
- advised the Ministry of Health on the services needed by children with disabilities

All of these activities are part of Los Pipitos' dream to build a society that helps children with disabilities develop their full potential. Parents are the key to making this happen.

Chapter 16
Why Children Lose Their Vision and What We Can Do

When people confront health problems like blindness, they often look for physical and medical causes. These causes are important, and you can learn about them in this chapter. However, to prevent blindness in a community, we also have to look at the social causes of blindness. For example, poor children are more likely to have eye infections and difficulty seeing than other children. Why?

The Story of Penda and Kesi

Penda lives in a small village in Africa. Several years ago, her husband died in a bus accident, leaving her with 3 young children. A few months later, she had another baby, a girl named Kesi. To feed her 4 children, Penda had to work long hours, so she stopped breastfeeding early.

When Kesi was 1 year old, her left eye got swollen. Penda treated her daughter's eye with herb compresses, but Kesi's eye did not get better. A few days later, a thick liquid started coming out of Kesi's eye. Penda was very worried. She had no money for a doctor, so a friend took Penda and Kesi to see a health worker in another village.

The health worker told Penda that her daughter was not getting enough of the right foods, so her eyes were losing their sight. To have healthy eyes, she explained, children need to eat foods like green leafy vegetables, orange vegetables and orange fruits that have vitamin A, which keeps eyes healthy. The health worker treated Kesi with vitamin A capsules. It was too late to save the sight in Kesi's left eye, but the treatment was early enough to save the sight in Kesi's right eye.

Penda was thankful that some of her daughter's sight had been saved. Now, she wants to teach other mothers about how important vitamin A is for children's eyes. She and the health worker are planning a meeting for pregnant women and mothers of young children. Penda is hopeful that other mothers in her village can find low-cost ways to eat better and improve health for themselves and their children.

Why did Kesi lose her sight?

There are several causes:

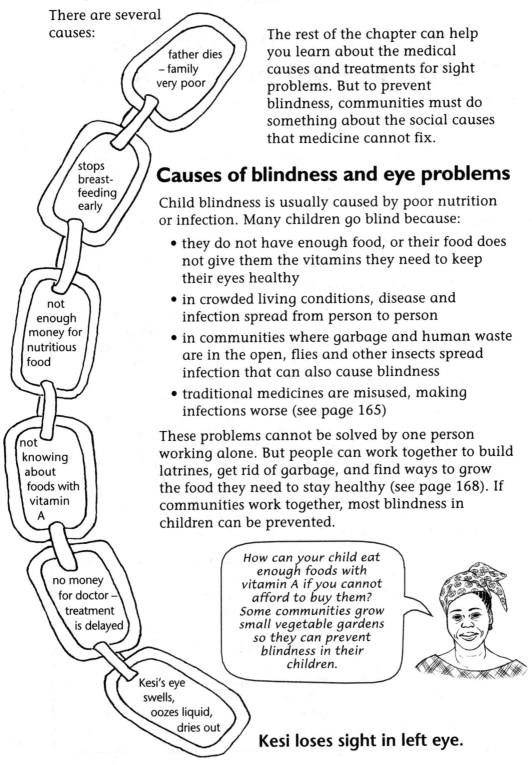

- father dies – family very poor
- stops breast-feeding early
- not enough money for nutritious food
- not knowing about foods with vitamin A
- no money for doctor – treatment is delayed
- Kesi's eye swells, oozes liquid, dries out

The rest of the chapter can help you learn about the medical causes and treatments for sight problems. But to prevent blindness, communities must do something about the social causes that medicine cannot fix.

Causes of blindness and eye problems

Child blindness is usually caused by poor nutrition or infection. Many children go blind because:

- they do not have enough food, or their food does not give them the vitamins they need to keep their eyes healthy
- in crowded living conditions, disease and infection spread from person to person
- in communities where garbage and human waste are in the open, flies and other insects spread infection that can also cause blindness
- traditional medicines are misused, making infections worse (see page 165)

These problems cannot be solved by one person working alone. But people can work together to build latrines, get rid of garbage, and find ways to grow the food they need to stay healthy (see page 168). If communities work together, most blindness in children can be prevented.

How can your child eat enough foods with vitamin A if you cannot afford to buy them? Some communities grow small vegetable gardens so they can prevent blindness in their children.

Kesi loses sight in left eye.

NIGHT BLINDNESS, DRY EYES, AND XEROPHTHALMIA (LACK OF VITAMIN A)

To keep the eyes healthy, people need to eat foods that have vitamin A, which is found in certain fruits, vegetables, and some meat. When a child eats enough foods with vitamin A, the surface of the eye stays wet and healthy. Many poor children do not get enough foods that are rich in vitamin A and their eyes begin to dry out. This is called "dry eyes."

Dark yellow and dark green vegetables, and some red or orange fruits and vegetables, are rich in vitamin A. Fish, milk, eggs, and liver also contain vitamin A.

Not getting enough vitamin A is the most common cause of blindness in children, especially in Africa and South Asia. It usually happens to children who are between 6 months and 6 years old. Children under 6 months who only breastfeed usually get enough vitamin A from their mother's milk.

Signs:

1. First, a child has trouble seeing in the dark or does not want to play outside after dark.

2. Then, the eyes may begin to look dry. The white part becomes less shiny, starts to wrinkle, and forms small gray spots that look like soap bubbles (Bitot's spots).

3. Later, the colored part of the eye also gets dry and dull, and may have little pits.

4. Finally, the colored part may get soft, swell, or burst, causing blindness.

Treatment:

- Give 3 doses of vitamin A. The first dose should be given as soon as you find out your child has 'night blindness' or 'dry eyes'. Give the second dose the next day, then a third dose 14 days later.

In the chart below, one capsule contains 50,000 IU (international units) of vitamin A.

Age	Number of capsules in one dose
under 6 months ....1 capsule	
6 months to 1 year ....2 capsules	
more than 1 year ....4 capsules	

Note: Once a child loses some of her sight, treatment will not get back that part of her sight. But starting treatment right away can keep her from losing any more of her sight.

Prevention:

- Breastfeed your children as long as possible — at least for 1 year, but even longer if you can.
- Try to make sure your child eats food rich in vitamin A every day.
- If a child is sick with measles, try to give her extra foods with vitamin A.

MEASLES (RUBEOLA)

Measles is a sickness that passes from person to person. If a child is already weak from not eating enough good foods or from diarrhea, being sick with measles can make her lose some or all of her sight.

Signs of measles:

- fever, runny nose, and cough
- red eyes
- red rash all over the body

Treatment:

- Your child should rest, drink a lot, and eat healthy foods. If a baby cannot breastfeed, give her breast milk with a cup.
- Give one dose of vitamin A (see the chart at the top of this page) as soon as you find out your child has measles. This will prevent 'dry eyes.'
- Give rehydration drink for diarrhea (see next page). This will help replace the liquids and nutrients lost when a child has diarrhea.

2 ways to make rehydration drink

If you can, add half a cup of fruit juice, coconut water, or mashed ripe banana to either drink. These contain potassium, a mineral which helps a sick child accept more food and drink.

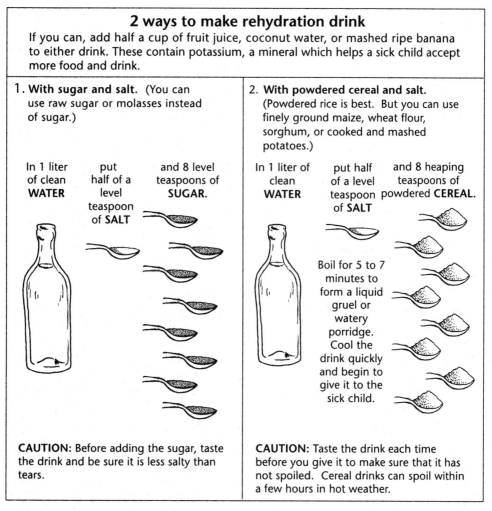

1. **With sugar and salt.** (You can use raw sugar or molasses instead of sugar.)

In 1 liter of clean **WATER** put half of a level teaspoon of **SALT** and 8 level teaspoons of **SUGAR.**

CAUTION: Before adding the sugar, taste the drink and be sure it is less salty than tears.

2. **With powdered cereal and salt.** (Powdered rice is best. But you can use finely ground maize, wheat flour, sorghum, or cooked and mashed potatoes.)

In 1 liter of clean **WATER** put half of a level teaspoon of **SALT** and 8 heaping teaspoons of powdered **CEREAL.**

Boil for 5 to 7 minutes to form a liquid gruel or watery porridge. Cool the drink quickly and begin to give it to the sick child.

CAUTION: Taste the drink each time before you give it to make sure that it has not spoiled. Cereal drinks can spoil within a few hours in hot weather.

Prevention:

- have your child immunized against measles. Your child can get the measles immunization as early as 6 to 9 months of age. See a health care worker to find out if this vaccine is available in your community.
- keep children away from anyone with measles.
- if someone has measles, wash their bedding, clothes, and eating tools separately from the rest of their family.

Usually, measles is not a serious sickness. But when children are weakened because they do not get enough to eat, or because of diarrhea from drinking unsafe water, sicknesses like measles can be very dangerous. It is really poverty that makes these children blind.

INFECTED EYES IN NEWBORN BABIES (NEONATAL CONJUNCTIVITIS)

> **All newborn babies should be protected from eye infections** by applying 1% tetracycline, erythromycin, or chloramphenicol eye ointment as soon as possible after birth. If these medicines are not available, you can also use a 2.5% solution of povidone-iodine.
>
> **Clean the baby's eyes with a clean cloth moistened with cool, boiled water. Pull down the lower lid of each eye, and put a little bit of ointment inside the lower lid. Putting ointment outside the eye does not do any good.**

If a baby gets an eye infection soon after birth, he can go blind. Eye infections can be caused by germs that get into the baby's eyes during birth, if the mother has an infection herself. The germs are from gonorrhea or chlamydia, which are infections that spread from one person to another during sex. Many people have these infections without knowing it because they have no signs of sickness. Because it is difficult to tell if a woman has an infection, it is important to treat all babies with eye ointment within a few hours after birth (see box above).

If a baby who is a few days old gets red, swollen eyes or has pus coming out of his eyes, he may have an eye infection and needs to be treated right away, whether or not he was given eye ointment after birth. The mother and her partner or partners should also be treated.

Signs of infection in a baby:

- red, swollen eyes
- pus in eyes
- lids matted shut, especially upon waking

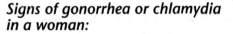

Signs of gonorrhea or chlamydia in a woman:

- yellow or green discharge from the vagina or anus
- pain or burning when passing urine
- fever
- pain in the lower belly
- pain or bleeding during sex
- or no signs at all

Remember even if the mother has no signs of infection, **if the baby has signs of infection then the baby needs to be treated.** The mother and her partner will also need treatment.

Treatment for the baby:

Pus should be cleaned from the eyes as soon as possible with a clean cloth and clean water.

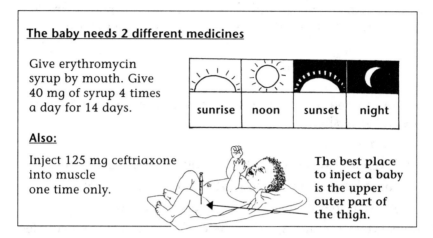

The baby needs 2 different medicines

Give erythromycin syrup by mouth. Give 40 mg of syrup 4 times a day for 14 days.

sunrise	noon	sunset	night

Also:

Inject 125 mg ceftriaxone into muscle one time only.

The best place to inject a baby is the upper outer part of the thigh.

If an infant has redness, swelling or pus in the eyes for more than 2 weeks, or these problems come and go for longer than 2 weeks, the baby may need more or different medicine. See a health worker.

Note: If your baby has lost some sight, the medicine will not help her get her sight back. But the medicine can help prevent her from losing more of her sight.

Treatment for the mother and her partner:

The mother and her partner need 2 different medicines

These are safe to take even if a woman is breastfeeding.

Take 500 mg of erythromycin by mouth 4 times a day for 7 days.

OR

Take 500 mg of amoxicillin 3 times a day for 10 days.

Also:

Take 400 mg of cefixime by mouth one time only.

OR

Inject 250 mg ceftriaxone into muscle one time only.

When women cannot speak with their partners about using condoms and protecting their sexual health, they risk becoming infected with gonorrhea and chlamydia. If more women were able to protect themselves, fewer babies would go blind.

TRACHOMA

Trachoma is a disease that is spread by flies. Once a person is infected, the disease gets worse slowly, usually over many years, unless it is treated. Trachoma is most common in poor, crowded living conditions, where there is little access to clean water.

Signs:

1. Trachoma begins with red, watery, sore eyes. But sometimes there are no early signs.
2. After about a month:
   - small yellowish-white or pink-gray dots form inside the upper eyelids
   - the top edge of the colored part of the eye may look cloudy
   - the white upper part of the eye gets a little red
3. Years later, the lumps inside the eyelids begin to go away, leaving white scars. These scars may pull the eyelashes down into the eye, scratching it and eventually causing blindness.

Treatment:

To learn how to put medicine in the eye, see page 160.

Put 1% tetracycline or erythromycin eye ointment inside both eyes 3 times each day.   **OR**   Use 3% tetracycline or erythromycin eye ointment 1 time each day.

Do this for 30 days. Put this ointment in the eyes of other children in the house, too.

For severe cases of trachoma, when the infection covers half or more of the inside of the eyelid, also give erythromycin by mouth for 14 days:

Age	Dose of erythromycin
under 3 years	75 to 150 mg 4 times a day, with food
3 to 7 years	150 mg 4 times a day, with food

Prevention:

Keep latrines covered and be strict about training your children to wash their hands with soap and water after they use the latrine.

CATARACTS

When a child has a cataract, the lens (a part of the eye just behind the black circle in the center) becomes white or milky. This causes a child to not see very well, as though everything were covered by a cloud. Cataracts may affect one or both eyes.

Cataracts are most common in older people. But some babies and children also get cataracts. Cataracts may be passed down in families (hereditary) or be caused by an eye injury. Often the cause of cataracts is unknown. Sometimes cataracts are caused by a German measles (rubella) infection during the first 3 months of pregnancy. Rubella can cause hearing loss as well as cataracts, so a child who has cataracts should also have his hearing tested. Cataracts are painless.

Signs:

- Blurred eyesight and a dimming of vision which get worse over time.
- The cataract may be seen from the outside. At first the center of the eye looks gray and then it becomes white.

Treatment:

Cataracts cannot be treated with medicine. An operation is needed to remove the cataract. After the operation, strong glasses may be needed.

Prevention:

- Pregnant women should stay away from people with German measles (rubella) or anyone sick with a fever and rash.
- Look for the signs of cataracts in children so they can be treated as early as possible.

RIVER BLINDNESS (ONCHOCERCIASIS)

River blindness is a disease caused by tiny worms that are spread by tiny black flies or "buffalo gnats." When the fly bites you, the worms carried by the fly get under your skin. If these worms get in the eye, they can cause blindness.

The black fly has a humped back and looks like this but is much smaller, like this

Signs:

- Lumps under the skin that slowly grow to a size of 2 to 6 cm (about 1 to 2½ inches).
- There may be itching when the baby worms are spreading.
- Pain in the back, shoulders, or hips (or pains all over).
- Skin changes. The skin on the back or belly may become thicker, darker, or scaly. Later, the skin becomes wrinkled, like the skin of an old person.
- Eye problems. First the eyes get red and watery, then very painful and itchy. Next, the center of the eye gets dull and pitted, as in 'dry eyes' (see page 157). Finally, the person becomes blind.

Treatment:

Some of the medicines used to treat river blindness may be harmful for children and should only be given by a health worker. Try to take your child to a health worker as soon as the first signs of river blindness appear. If treated early, your child can be cured.

Prevention:

- Black flies usually breed near fast-running water. Cleaning brush and vegetation back from the banks of fast-running streams may help reduce the number of flies.
- Avoid sleeping out-of-doors — especially in the daytime, which is when the flies usually bite. Mosquito nets can keep the flies away from you while you sleep.
- Cooperate with programs for the control of black flies.
- Watch for the signs of river blindness in children so they can get treatment as soon as possible.

EYE INJURIES

Many chemicals in the house — like acid, lye, and cleaning solutions — are common causes of eye problems in children. If one of these chemicals gets in the eye, immediately rinse the eye with cool, clean water for 15 to 20 minutes, and see a health worker right away.

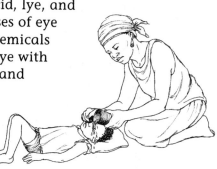

Be careful not to get water in the other eye. Tilt the child's head to the side and put the eye you are washing closest to the ground.

Injuries to the eye or scrapes on the eye can also cause blindness or problems seeing. Keep all sharp pointed objects, and also chemicals, out of the reach of children and keep play areas safe by removing objects that could cause eye injury. Warn children about the danger of throwing things at other people, or of throwing closed bottles, cans, or bullets into the fire. Also warn them about local plants and medicines that can injure the eyes.

Traditional beliefs and eye medicines

People have different traditional beliefs about what causes blindness. Some people believe that a child is blind because the parents have done something wrong. Others believe that a "black witch moth" flew by the baby's face, causing her to be blind. And some people think that a child is blind because someone has done evil to the child's mother and the child is "witched." None of these cause blindness.

There are traditional medicines which can help treat eye problems. But before using any medicine, traditional or modern, make sure that the medicine cannot harm the person in any way. Here are some general things to remember about traditional cures for health problems:

- The more cures there are to treat the same problem, the less likely it is that any of them will help.
- Disgusting cures rarely help people.
- Never use human or animal excrement as a cure. It can give the person an infection.
- The more the cure looks like or resembles the sickness, the more likely its benefits come only from the power of belief.

Eyes are fragile. It can be dangerous to put herbs and other materials in the eye because they can cause infections.

Other ways to prevent blindness

Keep your children's eyes clean. When
their eyes are infected or have pus,
clean them often with a clean cloth
wet with clean water. Anyone with an
eye infection should try to see a
health worker.

Eyes should not be touched if you or
your child has a cold sore anywhere.
The infection that causes cold sores
can cause blindness if it gets into the eye.

**Wipe each eye from the corner of
the eye by the nose to the corner
of the eye by the ear. Use a
different part of the cloth to
clean each eye.**

Women need to take special
care of themselves when they
are pregnant. They need to
have enough good food to eat.
A health worker can help
pregnant women learn how to:

- stay healthy
- prevent blindness in their
  babies by staying away
  from people with German
  measles (rubella)
- avoid using certain
  medicines

Health workers should promote
breastfeeding so women can pass
nutrition and immunities to their
children through their breast milk.

Health workers can also try to
get all children vaccinated
against infectious diseases like
measles (rubeola) and German
measles (rubella).

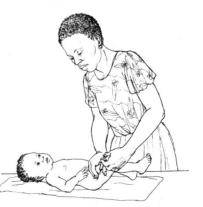

How can people work together to prevent blindness?

Go back to Penda's story at the beginning of this chapter. Look at the chain of causes that led to her baby losing sight in one eye. How could the story have been changed to have a happier ending? How can people in your community change the conditions that make children go blind when it could be prevented?

Gardening to prevent blindness

In Bangladesh, thousands of children go blind every year because they do not eat enough foods that have vitamin A. Delwara Hasina lives in a village in Bangladesh with her husband and 3 children. Although Mrs. Hasina has no blind children in her own family, she and other people in her village decided to help prevent blindness. So she contacted Banchte Shekha, an organization of women helping other women in rural villages.

At Banchte Shekha, Mrs. Hasina learned that certain fruits and vegetables contain enough vitamin A to prevent blindness. She also got training on how to grow vegetables from Banchte Shekha workers who had been trained earlier by Helen Keller International, an organization that works the world over to prevent blindness. Now Mrs. Hasina grows vegetables on a small plot (30 square meters) next to her home and on another plot the same size next to her parents' home.

"Before, our gardening was seasonal and we grew only a few things like bottle gourd and beans," Mrs. Hasina said. "Now, we grow more than 10 varieties of vegetables, spices, and fruits all year round." She and other women are encouraging families to start gardens. It does not take much space to grow enough vegetables with vitamin A for a family. "I cook some of my family's daily meal from the garden," she says. "My children like red amaranth (lal shak) and Indian spinach, which I grow throughout the year."

Mrs. Hasina sells her extra produce in the local village market. She uses the money to buy additional food and educational materials for her children. "The amount of money is small, but it helps me to meet the children's needs," she said.

Mrs. Hasina's garden is one of more than 600,000 household gardens in Bangladesh that are part of this international gardening project. See page 188 for information about how to contact Helen Keller International and start gardens in your community.

Chapter 17

As Your Child Gets Older

When your child realizes he is blind

A young child who is blind thinks that everyone learns about the world the same way he does. He is not aware that other children have different ways of knowing and learning about the world. But, as he gets older, a child who is blind begins to understand that he is different.

A young child who is blind thinks that other people look at things with their hands, too.

Mama, look at what I did.

Look at the fruits on the tree.

How can Kado see the fruits without climbing the tree?

When a blind child is around 5 years old, he begins to understand that other children do not need to touch something to "look" at it.

As he begins to notice that he is different, he may have new, strong feelings about his difference. Some children who are blind or cannot see well feel sad about their difference. Other children are angry or frustrated.

Mama, how come Kado can see the fruits and I can't?

Helping your child with his feelings

Many blind children feel upset, frustrated or sad when they notice
they are blind and cannot do all the things other children can do. If
you are part of a parents group, other parents may be able to tell you
how they answer their children's questions. It may help you to talk
about it ahead of time so you can be ready for your child's questions.

When you were a little baby, Carlos, you got very sick, and since then you haven't been able to see well.

A blind child may express his feelings by insisting that he wants to see, or by insisting that he will be able to see when he gets bigger. He may ask you why he is blind.

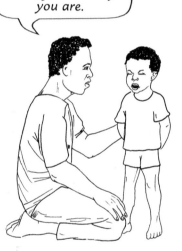

Essien, I am very proud of all the things you can do. And I love you very much, just the way you are.

Your child may become really angry and he may show his anger by his behavior and the way he acts with his family.

As you answer your child's questions, reassure him and praise him for all the things he can do. If he knows he is cared for and his feelings are understood, it will be easier for him to accept his blindness.

When your child talks about these feelings, tell him you understand that he is upset. Let him know that you care about the way he feels.

I know you're feeling sad because you'd like to see the fruit that Kado can see.

Balancing dependence and independence

Children like to do things that make them feel capable. A child who is old enough to notice he is blind may also notice other children his age are doing things that he would like to do, but cannot. He may feel frustrated that he is not allowed to be as independent as he wants to be.

When there is no danger, give your child as much independence as you can so he will learn to do as much as he can by himself. Like other children, your child who is blind needs to be able to take care of himself.

I can pick beans just like my big brother does.

Even when he is grown up, your child will sometimes have to ask for help from a person who can see. Teach your child that everyone asks for help sometimes.

Chen, the basket is heavy, and the ground is so bumpy. Could you please carry my basket?

No thank you, Grandma. I'm a big girl. I can put my shirt on by myself.

Sometimes people offer unwanted help. Teach your child that accepting help is her choice. She can simply say "No, thank you" when she feels she can do something by herself.

Continuing to solve problems

As your child grows older, he will find new challenges to overcome. It is important to remember that:

You and your child are the experts when it comes to **what works for him**. You understand his abilities and his personality. You and he have worked out ways to do things.

I think I can tell which beans aren't good. They feel softer. Let me try and you tell me if I'm right.

OK. Put the bad beans on the cloth and the good beans in the basket. I'll check on how you're doing.

Now that your child is older, he can solve some problems by himself. He can think of his own ways to do things.

If I wash one pan at a time and put the clean pans on my left side, I won't have to worry that the pans will float away. I'll also know which pans have been washed.

Other people who cannot see well have figured out lots of special ways of doing things. Your child can learn many helpful things from other people who cannot see well.

I fold money differently depending how much it is worth. That way I can tell by touch what the value of each one is.

Thinking about the future

Your child may only be 5 years old now, but soon he will be a big boy, and someday he will be a grown man. You can help your child set high goals for himself. He can grow up to be an independent adult. Help him see himself as capable, and have a realistic attitude about his blindness. Blind adults learn many skills. They work, get married, have children, and are good parents.

Using your experience to help others

As he grows up, both you and your child will learn a lot about the different ways children who are blind can learn to do things. Sharing your experience with parents who have babies who are blind or cannot see well will be a great help to them.

Your grown child may also decide to use his experience to help children who are blind or who cannot see well. It is very good for little children who are blind to spend time with adults who are also blind or cannot see well.

You may be able to work with other people to organize for better support and better services for parents of blind children. Most important, you can work to change the conditions of poverty so there will be less blindness in the future.

Your grown son or daughter may choose to work with other people to improve school programs and work opportunities for blind children and adults.

Appendix A
Child Development Charts

How to use these child development charts

Children develop in several main areas: **physical** (body), **mental** (mind), **communication** (gesturing or talking), and **social** (relating to other people). Some skills a child learns include all these areas. For example, when a child reaches her arms up to be held, she is using a:

- physical skill – she holds up her arms
- mental skill – she recognizes you
- communication skill – she tells you what she wants
- social skill – she enjoys being held by you

The charts on pages 178 to 183 show some of the skills children learn and when most children learn them. You can use the chart to get general information about how children develop and to help you decide what skills your child needs to learn.

| 6 months | 12 months | 2 years |

The charts show how children's physical skills change as children grow.

▶ *To help you decide what skills your child needs to learn*

Find the chart for the age group closest to your child's age. On the chart, circle the skills your child has. You may find your child does not have some skills that other children his age have. Knowing this can help you decide which activities you want to work on with your child.

If your child is behind

Use this book as a guide. Each chapter in the book explains more about these skills and the order in which skills need to be learned. **It is important to work on the skills your child needs to learn next, not the skills other children his age are learning.** Trying to teach a child skills before he is ready will lead to disappointment for both you and your child.

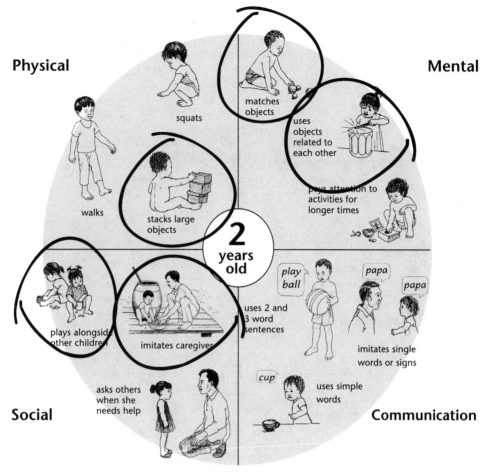

Physical

squats

walks

stacks large
objects

Mental

matches
objects

uses
objects
related to
each other

pays attention to
activities for
longer times

**2
years
old**

play
ball

papa

papa

uses 2 and
3 word
sentences

imitates single
words or signs

Social

plays alongside
other children

imitates caregiver

asks others
when she
needs help

cup

uses simple
words

Communication

In the chart above, a mother has circled the skills her 20-month-old
daughter can do. Her child needs activities to help her gain physical
and communication skills.

Look first in the chapters that focus on the skills you want to teach
your child, but you will find useful information in other chapters as well.

Chapter → Area of Development ↓	Activities for the Young Baby	Communication	Thinking Skills	Teaching Everyday Activities	Movement	Helping Your Child Know Where She Is	Becoming Part of the Community	Getting Ready for Child-care and School
	5	6	7	8	10	11	13	14
Physical	●			●	●	●	●	
Mental	●		●			●		●
Social	●			●			●	●
Communication	●	●					●	

Each part of this circle shows a different area of development. The pictures and words are examples of skills that many babies have when they are **3 months old.**

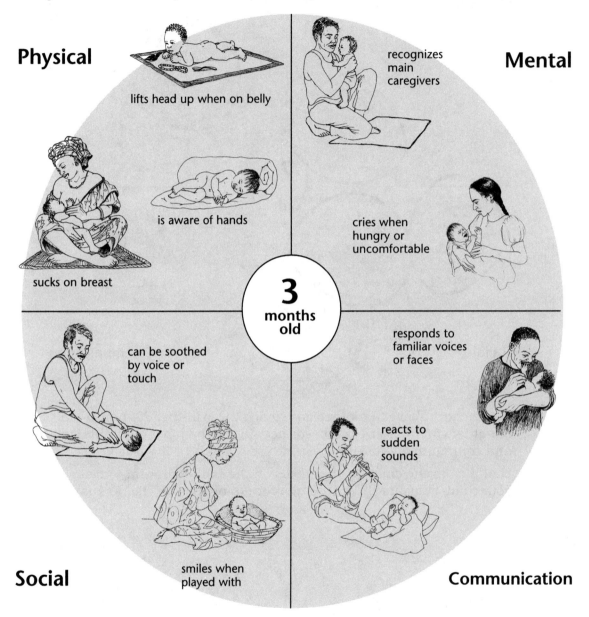

Physical

lifts head up when on belly

is aware of hands

sucks on breast

Mental

recognizes main caregivers

cries when hungry or uncomfortable

3 months old

can be soothed by voice or touch

responds to familiar voices or faces

reacts to sudden sounds

Social

smiles when played with

Communication

Babies who cannot do 2 skills in any part of the circle will benefit from activities that help babies develop in that area, but the pictures are only **examples** of skills. For example, in the Communication part of the circle: You do not have to play the flute! The question to ask yourself is if your baby reacts to a sudden sound.

Keep in mind that a baby will learn best by doing activities that other babies the same age do in your community.

Each part of this circle shows a different area of development. The pictures and words are examples of skills that many babies have when they are **6 months old**.

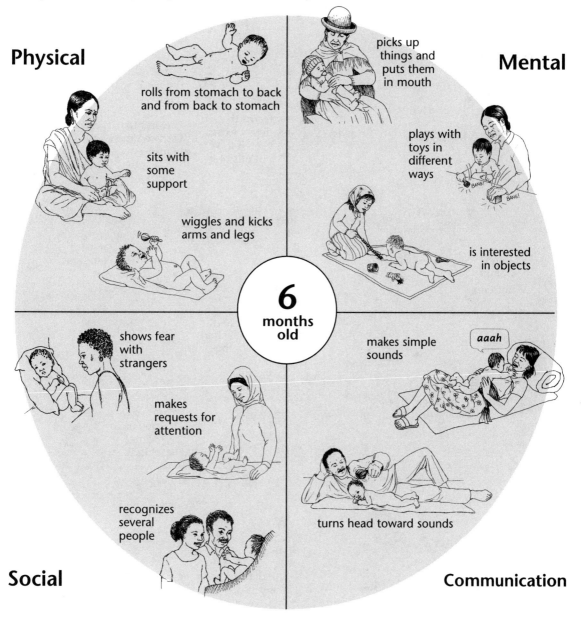

Physical

rolls from stomach to back and from back to stomach

sits with some support

wiggles and kicks arms and legs

Mental

picks up things and puts them in mouth

plays with toys in different ways

is interested in objects

6 months old

Social

shows fear with strangers

makes requests for attention

recognizes several people

Communication

makes simple sounds

aaah

turns head toward sounds

Babies who cannot do 2 skills in any part of the circle will benefit from activities that help babies develop in that area, but the pictures are only **examples** of skills. For example, in the Physical part of the circle: Your baby does not have to play with a rattle. The question to ask yourself is if your baby wiggles and kicks.

Keep in mind that a baby will learn best by doing activities that other babies the same age do in your community.

Each part of this circle shows a different area of development. The pictures and words are examples of skills that many babies have when they are **12 months old**.

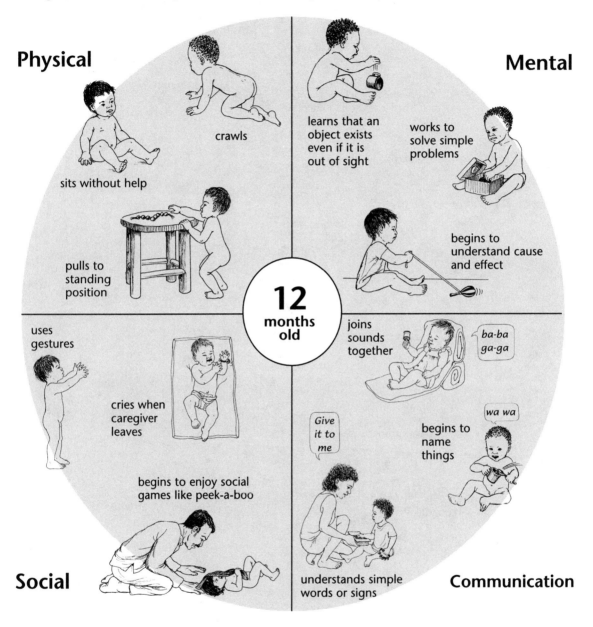

Babies who cannot do 2 skills in any part of the circle will benefit from activities that help babies develop in that area, but the pictures are only **examples** of skills. For example, in the Social part of the circle: You do not have to play peek-a-boo with your baby. The question to ask yourself is if your baby enjoys social games.

Keep in mind that a baby will learn best by doing activities that other babies the same age do in your community.

Each part of this circle shows a different area of development. The pictures and words are examples of skills that many children have when they are **2 years old**.

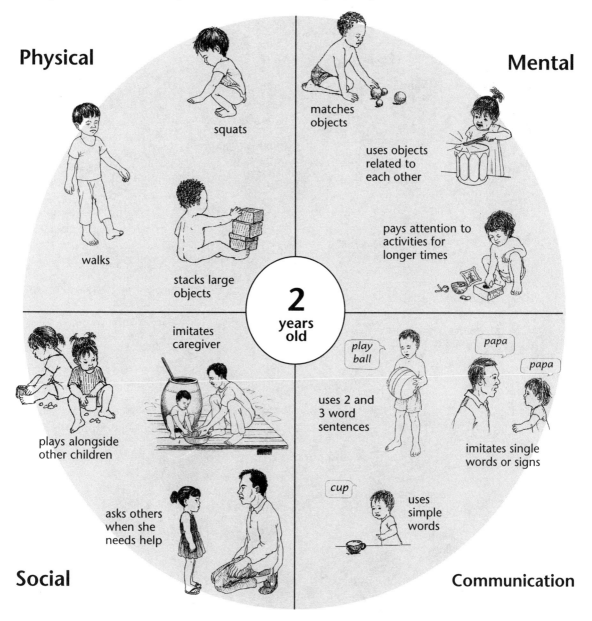

Children who cannot do 2 skills in any part of the circle will benefit from activities that help children develop in that area, but the pictures are only **examples** of skills. For example, in the Mental part of the circle: Your child does not have to be able to play a drum. The question to ask yourself is if your child uses 2 objects together.

Keep in mind that a child will learn best by doing activities that other children the same age do in your community.

Each part of this circle shows a different area of development. The pictures and words are examples of skills that many children have when they are **3 years old.**

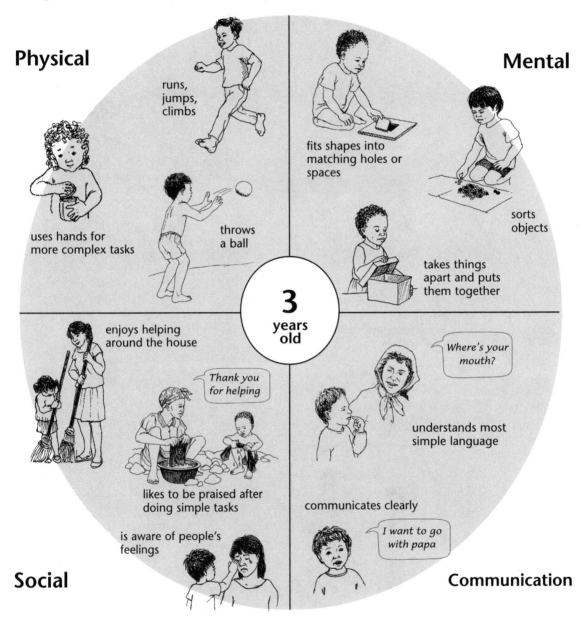

Children who cannot do 2 skills in any part of the circle will benefit from activities that help children develop in that area, but the pictures re only **examples** of skills. For example, in the Social part of the circle: Your child does not have to sweep the floor. The question to ask yourself is if your child enjoys helping work with the family.

Keep in mind that a child will learn best by doing activities that other children the same age do in your community.

Each part of this circle shows a different area of development. The pictures and words are examples of skills that many children have when they are **5 years old.**

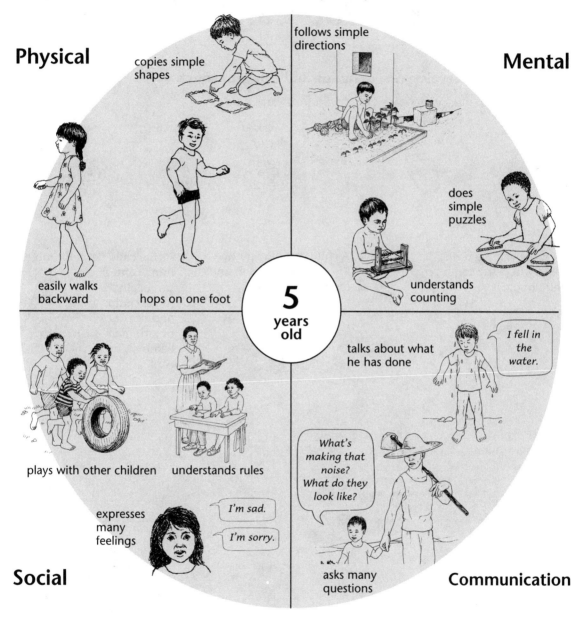

Physical

copies simple shapes

easily walks backward

hops on one foot

Mental

follows simple directions

does simple puzzles

understands counting

5 years old

talks about what he has done

I fell in the water.

Social

plays with other children

understands rules

expresses many feelings

I'm sad.

I'm sorry.

Communication

What's making that noise? What do they look like?

asks many questions

Children who cannot do 2 skills in any part of the circle will benefit from activities that help children develop in that area, but the pictures are only **examples** of skills. For example, in the Social part of the circle: Your child does not have to be listening to a teacher. The question to ask yourself is if your child understands rules like other children do.

Keep in mind that a child will learn best by doing activities that other children the same age do in your community.

Appendix B
Toys You Can Make

Toys that help develop use of hands and sense of touch

You can make beads and chains out of wild fruits and nuts.

| prickly | rough and smooth | fuzzy | wrinkled or lumpy | smooth | wriggly |

For a baby, hang a ring of beads where she can reach and handle it.

A child can play putting the nuts and pods in and out of a container.

Later he can learn to sort them.

As the child develops more hand control, she can begin to make chains and necklaces by stringing beads on a cord.

'Snakes' can be made by stringing nuts, 'caps' of acorns, bottle caps, or any combination of things.

small green mango (or whatever you can think of)

bottle caps

beans for 'rattle' of rattlesnake

If you use your imagination, there are all kinds of toy animals you and your children can have fun making.

'Hedgehogs'

papache (woody fruits from wild bush)

guasima fruit

acorn

knobby sticks from papache bush

cloves

Rattles and other noise toys

Gourd rattle

Find a small gourd (wild gourds or tree gourds may work).

Cut a round hole at the stem and clean out the seeds and flesh. Let it dry out well.

Put 2 or 3 small rocks, nuts or other objects inside.

Find a stick the size of the hole. If the hole is large, thin down this part of the stick.

Glue the stick to the gourd.

Glue here.

To make it stronger and better looking, mix white glue and sawdust, fill in here, and after the glue dries, sand it smooth.

Paint it colorfully.

Plastic bottle rattle

a see-through plastic bottle

stick of wood

ring cut from a plastic bottle, bamboo or whatever you have

strips cut from plastic bottles of different colors, colorful stones, nuts, etc.

ring can be wrapped with strips of cloth or tire tubing for easier grip

Bamboo rattle

SIMPLE FORM

cork or plug

WITH HANDLE

Tin can rattle

Cowhorn rattle

Trim rough edges.

Put in a cardboard or wood plug.

small rocks

Then seal with a mix of sawdust and white glue, or plaster of Paris.

glue

sawdust

Smooth the surface and let it dry.

Ideas for homemade music

gourds with seeds in them

2 wood sticks

tambourine

can lids

jingle bells

can lids

jingle bells

marimba

loose hardwood plates

castanets (wooden clappers)

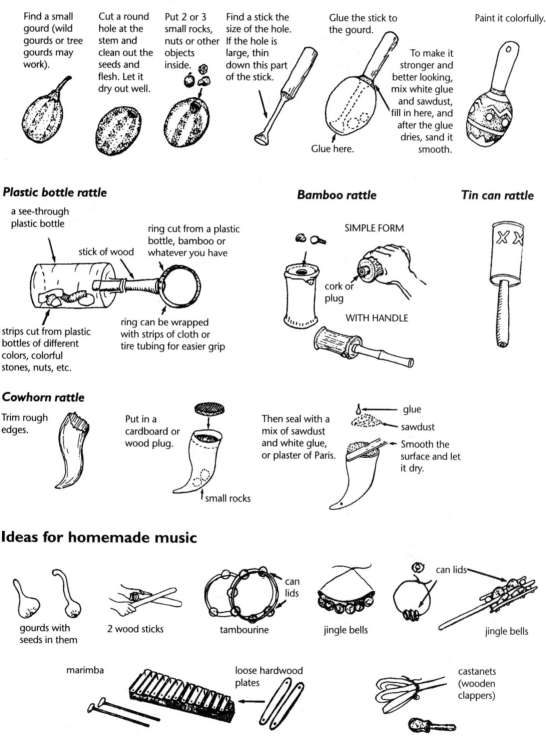

Soft rattle

Use a small can or bottle with a small stone inside...

...or use 2 small bells.

Cut a colorful soft cloth (flannel) into this shape.

Sew it into a square and turn inside out.

Place can or bells in cloth square and pack wild kapok, cotton or bits of sponge around it. Sew it shut.

wild kapok

Doll rattle

Draw a doll on 2 pieces of cloth, and cut them out.

Sew the 2 dolls together.

Turn the doll inside out.

Leave a small opening.

Put small bells or a rattle inside and stuff with kapok, cotton or sponge and sew shut.

Sew or draw on a face.

Animal rattles

can be made in the same way.

Ball rattle

Cut 3 pieces of one color...

...and 3 pieces of another color.

Sew them together except for a small hole. Turn inside out and stuff.

Push-along noise toy

Make hole in lid and bottom of tin.

Put bottle tops, small stones, etc. inside.

Put loop of stiff wire through holes with knot inside tin.

Bamboo push-along

Cut here

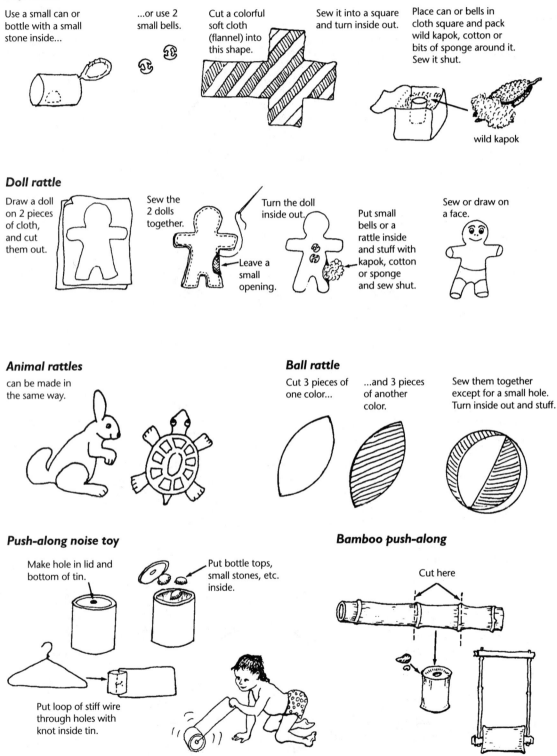

Games fitting pegs or blocks into holes

These games help develop better hand control and 'hand-eye coordination.' They also help the child learn to compare sizes, shapes, and color.

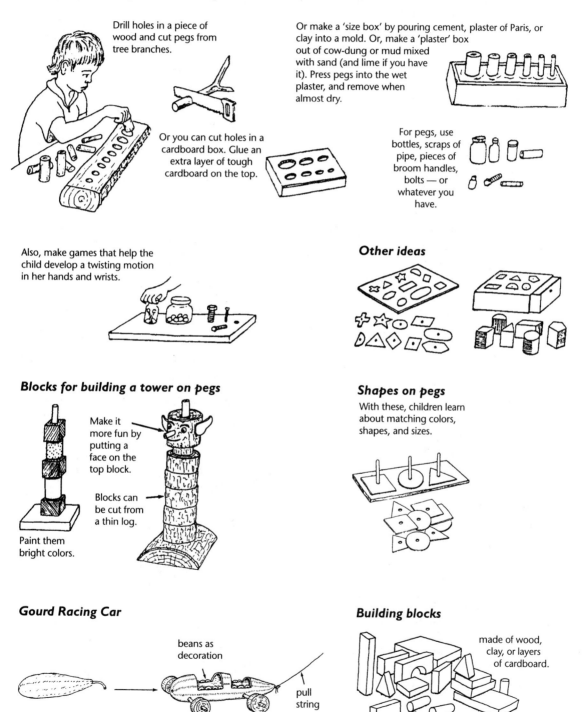

Drill holes in a piece of wood and cut pegs from tree branches.

Or make a 'size box' by pouring cement, plaster of Paris, or clay into a mold. Or, make a 'plaster' box out of cow-dung or mud mixed with sand (and lime if you have it). Press pegs into the wet plaster, and remove when almost dry.

Or you can cut holes in a cardboard box. Glue an extra layer of tough cardboard on the top.

For pegs, use bottles, scraps of pipe, pieces of broom handles, bolts — or whatever you have.

Also, make games that help the child develop a twisting motion in her hands and wrists.

Other ideas

Blocks for building a tower on pegs

Make it more fun by putting a face on the top block.

Blocks can be cut from a thin log.

Paint them bright colors.

Shapes on pegs

With these, children learn about matching colors, shapes, and sizes.

Gourd Racing Car

beans as decoration

pull string

Building blocks

made of wood, clay, or layers of cardboard.

Where to Get More Information

Here is a small selection of organizations and printed materials that can provide useful information about blindness and young children. We have tried to list organizations and materials covering as many of the topics in this book as possible, and to include groups working in all areas of the world. Many of the printed materials are easy to adapt and often include other helpful resource lists.

ORGANIZATIONS

Blind Babies Foundation
5016 Mission Street
San Francisco, California 94112, USA
phone: (1) 415-586-6140
fax: (1) 415-586-6279
e-mail: bbfinfo@blindbabies.org
http://www.blindbabies.org
Source of materials and publications, videos, and fact sheets for families with infants and young children who are blind.

Christoffel Blindenmission International (CBMI)
Nibelungenstrasse 124, D-64625
Bensheim, Germany
phone: (49) 6251-131-0; fax: (49) 6251-131-165
e-mail: overseas@cbm-i.org
http://www.cbmi.org
Operates eye units, mobile eye-care services, village health centers, schools, and training institutions in 94 countries.

Helen Keller International
USA: 90 West Street, 2nd floor
New York, New York 10006, USA
phone: (1) 212-766-5266
Africa: P.O. Box 11728, Niamey, Niger
e-mail: hkiniger@intnet.ne
phone: (227) 75-33-14
Asia: Jl. Bungur Dalam 23A
Kemang, Jakarta 12730, Indonesia
phone: (62) 21-719-8147
Trains local partners in developing community gardening projects to grow vegetables and fruits to prevent blindness.

Hilton/Perkins Program
Perkins School for the Blind
175 N. Beacon St.
Watertown, Massachusetts 02472, USA
phone: (1) 617-972-7220; fax: (1) 617-923-8076
e-mail: collinsm@perkins.pvt.k12.ma.us
Provides technical assistance and support for the development of programs for multi-handicapped blind and deaf-blind children in developing countries.

Lighthouse International
111 East 59 Street
New York, New York 10022, USA
phone in the USA: 800-829-0500
phone outside the USA: (1) 212-821-9200
fax: 212-821-9707
e-mail: info@lighthouse.org
http://www.lighthouse.org
Many useful on-line English language publications.

National Association for the Blind (NAB)
11 Khan Abdul Gaffar Khan Road
Worli Sea Face, Mumbai 400 025, India
phone: (91) 22-493-6930
http://www.commercenetindia.com/nab/
Branches in 18 States and 64 Districts in India, providing education, rehabilitation, training, and residential programs.

PLAN International
Chobham House
Christchurch Way, Woking
Surrey GU21 1JG, UK
phone: (44) 1483-755155
fax: (44) 1483-756505
Works directly with communities and families in 40 countries, providing material aid and services. PLAN's child sponsorship program supports about 1 million children.

Royal National Institute for the Blind (RNIB)
224 Great Portland Street
London W1N 6AA, UK
phone: (44) 020-7388-1266
fax: (44) 020-7388-2034
e-mail: helpline@rnib.org.uk
http://www.rnib.org.uk
Many on-line publications and useful links. The RNIB also produces an international database with detailed information about agencies for people who are blind:
http://www.tiresias.org/agencies/agencies_a.htm

Sight Savers International
Grosvenor Hall, Bolnore Road, Haywards Heath
West Sussex RH16 4BX, UK
phone: (44) 4-446600
fax: (44) 4-446685
e-mail: scastle@sightsaversint.org.uk
http://www.sightsavers.org.uk
Works with local partners in 25 countries, providing eye care, cataract surgery, education, and training.

World Blind Union
ONCE – La Coruña, 18
28020 Madrid, Spain
phone: (34-1) 571-36-85; fax: (34-1) 571-57-77
e-mail: umc@once.es; http://umc.once.es
Has member organizations in most countries, with programs in rehabilitation, education, training, health care, and income generation.

PRINTED MATERIALS

An Orientation and Mobility Primer for Families and Young Children
Dodson-Burke, Bonnie, and Hill, Everett W.
American Foundation for the Blind
P.O. Box 1020
Sewickley, Pennsylvania 15143 USA
phone in USA: 800-232-3044
phone outside the USA: (1) 412-741-0609
fax: (1) 412-741-0609

Blindness and Early Childhood Development
Warren, David H.
American Foundation for the Blind *(see address above)*

Children With Visual Impairments: A parents' guide
Holbrook, M. Cay, editor   (395 pages, 1995)
Woodbine House, Inc.
6510 Bells Mill Rd.
Bethesda, Maryland 20817, USA
This book provides parents with guidance and support in caring for their child with a visual impairment. It covers such topics as diagnosis and treatment, family adjustment, child development, early intervention and special education, mobility and orientation, multiple disabilities, and thinking about the future.

Dancing Cheek to Cheek
Meyers, Laura, and Lansky, Pamela
(33 pages, 1991)
Blind Childrens Center
P.O. Box 29159
4120 Marathon St.
Los Angeles, California 90029, USA
phone in USA: 800-222-3566;
phone outside USA: (1) 323-664-2153
fax: (1) 323-655-3828
e-mail: info@blindchildrenscenter.org
Explores nurturing strategies for fostering early social interactions, language development, and play.

Disabled Village Children: A guide for community health workers, rehabilitation workers, and families
Werner, David   (654 pages, 1999)
The Hesperian Foundation
1919 Addison St., Suite 304
Berkeley, California 94704, USA
phone in USA: 888-729-1796
phone outside the USA: (1) 510-845-4507
fax: (1) 510-845-0539
e-mail: bookorders@hesperian.org
http://www.hesperian.org

Early Years, a Series
Royal National Institute for the Blind
American Foundation for the Blind *(see address above)*
These booklets provide important information on caring for children who are visually impaired from birth to age 10 years. The booklets include information about medical terms and health professionals, caregiving advice, information for educational professionals working with children who are visually impaired, play and the visually impaired child, information on the importance of mobility education.

Fathers: A Common Ground
Armenta-Schmitt, Fernanda (50 pages, 1998)
Blind Childrens Center *(see address above)*
Investigates the role that fathers play and the concerns of fathers in raising children who are visually impaired.

First Steps: A handbook for teaching young children who are visually impaired
Blind Childrens Center *(see address above)*
203 pages, 1993
Written in easy to understand language, this handbook is for both parents and professionals who care for children with vision problems. Strategies for teaching are also explored.

**Get a Wiggle On: A guide for helping
visually impaired children grow**
>Raynor, Sherry & Drouillard, Richard
(80 pages, 1996)
Blind Children's Fund
4740 Okemos Road
Okemos, Michigan 48864-1637, USA
phone: (1) 517-347-1357
fax: (1) 517-347-1459
e-mail: blindchfnd@aol.com

>*One of the most useful and parent-friendly
books on early intervention.*

**Guidelines and Games for Teaching
Efficient Braille Reading**
>Olson, M.R. and Mangold, S. (1981)
American Foundation for the Blind *(see
address above)*

>*Written primarily for teachers, but has
valuable information for parents. Includes
preschool activities that provide a foundation
for reading in Braille.*

How to Raise a Blind Child
>Fichtner, Dorothea (64 pages, 1979)
Christoffel Blindenmission,
Nibelungenstrasse 124
D-6140 Bensheim 4, Germany

**How to Thrive, Not Just Survive: A guide to
independent skills for blind and visually
impaired children and youth**
>Swallow, R. and Huebner, K.M. (1987)
American Foundation for the Blind *(see
address above)*

>*This book was written for parents and focuses
on teaching practical skills to children with
vision problems.*

**Learning Together: A parent guide to
socially based routines for visually
impaired infants**
>Chen, Deborah, Friedman, Clare T., and
Calvello, Gail (44 pages, 1990)
American Printing House for the Blind
P.O. Box 6085
Louisville, Kentucky 40206-0085, USA
phone in the USA: 800-223-1839
phone outside the USA: (1) 502-895-2405
e-mail: aph@iglou.com

**Learning to Play: Common concerns for
the visually impaired preschool child**
>Recchia, Susan (12 pages, 1987)
Blind Childrens Center *(see address above)*

>*Presents play activities for pre-school children
who are visually impaired.*

**Lessons With a Child Who Is Blind:
Development and early intervention in the
first years of life**
>Brambring, Michael (147 pages, 1993)
Blind Children's Fund *(see address above)*

>*This tells the story of a family's experiences
raising a daughter who is blind and the
support they received from an early
intervention professional. Letters between the
family and the professional document the
child's development.*

Move It!
>Latham, M.D. (1977)
Blind Childrens Fund *(see address above)*

>*An excellent follow-up to "Get a Wiggle On,"
this booklet contains more helpful hints for
parents.*

Move With Me
>Hug, Doris; Chernus-Mansfield, Nancy,
and Hayashi, Dori (12 pages, 1987)
Blind Childrens Center *(see address above)*

>*How to foster the development of movement
in babies who are visually impaired.*

**Reaching, Crawling, Walking...Let's Get
Moving**
>Simmons, Susan, and O'Maida, Sharon
(24 pages, 1993)
Blind Childrens Center *(see address above)*

>*Strategies for supporting mobility and
fostering orientation in preschool children
who are visually impaired.*

**Parenting Preschoolers: Suggestions for
raising young blind and visually impaired
children**
>Ferrell, Kay Alicyn (28 pages, 1984)
American Foundation for the Blind *(see
address above)*

>*This book gives practical advice about caring
for children who are visually impaired and
provides answers to commonly asked
questions. Ideas on how to adapt a child's
environment to meet her needs and how to
choose an early education program are also
included.*

Reach Out and Teach: Meeting the training needs of parents of visually and multiply handicapped young children

Ferrell, Kay Alicyn (176 pages, 1985)
American Foundation for the Blind *(see address above)*

This book gives parents strategies to encourage their child's motor and cognitive development. A workbook gives parents a way to record information about their child's responses and development.

Show Me How: A manual for parents of preschool visually impaired and blind children

Brennan, Mary (56 pages, 1982)
American Foundation for the Blind *(see address above)*

This book provides parents and professionals with strategies for helping visually impaired pre-school children reach age-appropriate goals, foster social relationships, improve motor skills and sensory awareness, and learn skills for daily living.

Standing On My Own Two Feet

La Prelle, Lori Lynne (36 pages, 1996)
Blind Childrens Center *(see address above)*

A guide to simple construction of mobility devices for pre-school children who are visually impaired. Devices can be easily adapted to an individual's needs.

Talk to Me: A language guide for parents of blind children

Kekelis, Lee, and Chernus-Mansfield, Nancy (36 pages, 1996)
Blind Childrens Center *(see address above)*

Practical strategies for communication with a child who has vision problems.

OTHER BOOKS FROM THE HESPERIAN FOUNDATION

Where There Is No Doctor, by David Werner with Carol Thuman and Jane Maxwell, is perhaps the most widely used health care manual in the world. The book provides vital, easily understood information on how to diagnose, treat and prevent common diseases. Special importance is placed on ways to prevent health problems, including cleanliness, a healthy diet and vaccinations. The authors also emphasize the active role villagers must take in their own health care. 512 pages.

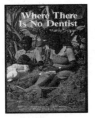

Where There Is No Dentist, by Murray Dickson shows people how to care for their own teeth and gums, and how to prevent tooth and gum problems. Emphasis is placed on sharing this knowledge in the home, community and school. The author also gives detailed and well-illustrated information on using dental equipment, placing fillings, taking out teeth, and suggests ways to teach dental hygiene and nutrition. 208 pages.

Disabled Village Children, by David Werner, contains a wealth of information about most common disabilities of children, including polio, cerebral palsy, juvenile arthritis, blindness and deafness. The author gives suggestions for simplified rehabilitation at the village level and explains how to make a variety of appropriate low-cost aids. Emphasis is placed on how to help disabled children find a role and be accepted in the community. 672 pages.

Helping Health Workers Learn, by David Werner and Bill Bower, is an indispensable resource for anyone involved in teaching about health. This heavily illustrated book shows how to make health education fun and effective. Includes activities for mothers and children; pointers for using theater, flannel-boards, and other techniques; and many ideas for producing low-cost teaching aids. Emphasizing a people-centered approach to health care, it presents strategies for effective community involvement through participatory education. 640 pages.

A Book for Midwives, by Susan Klein, is written for midwives, traditional birth attendants, community health workers and anyone concerned about the health of pregnant women and their babies. The book is an invaluable tool for midwives facilitating education and training sessions as well as an essential reference for practice. The author emphasizes helping pregnant women stay healthy; giving good care and dealing with complications during labor, childbirth and after birth; family planning; breastfeeding; and homemade, low-cost equipment. 528 pages.

Where Women Have No Doctor, by A.August Burns, Ronnie Lovich, Jane Maxwell and Katharine Shapiro, combines self-help medical information with an understanding of the ways poverty, discrimination, and cultural beliefs limit women's health and access to care. Clearly written and with over 1000 drawings, this book is an essential resource for any woman who wants to improve her health, and for health workers who want more information about the problems that affect only women, or that affect women differently from men. 584 pages.